M000282357

# Confessions

## A Memoir of Hope for the Suffering

## Lawrence Bowman

### WAYMAKER PUBLISHING

CONFESSIONS: A MEMOIR OF HOPE FOR THE SUFFERING

ISBN: 978-0-9988869-7-8

Copyright © 2024 by Waymaker Publishing
www.WaymakerPublishing.com

A special thanks to David Safford for his dedication and skill in helping bring this book to life. A special thanks to Brittney Ybarra for interior design of the book.

All scriptures are taken from the King James Bible.

All parts of this book may not be reproduced or transmitted in any form or by any means, electronic or mechanical, including photocopying, recording, or any information storage and retrieval system without the written permission from the author. For permission, please contact www.WaymakerPublishing.com.

For information regarding special discounts for bulk purchases, please contact the author.

**Follow Lawrence Bowman on Facebook.**

**Explore more inspiring content of Lawrence's at www.MissionFrontier.info/blog**

Printed in the United States of America.

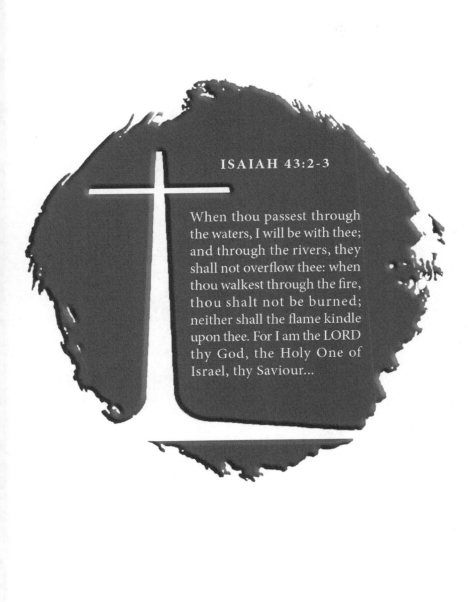

## ISAIAH 43:2-3

When thou passest through the waters, I will be with thee; and through the rivers, they shall not overflow thee: when thou walkest through the fire, thou shalt not be burned; neither shall the flame kindle upon thee. For I am the LORD thy God, the Holy One of Israel, thy Saviour...

# Contents

**Introduction**—Where Is God When I'm Suffering?        9

**One**—Broken Plans: God's Clever Trick        17

*Have You Considered:*
*Why Do I Still Suffer and Sin after Accepting Christ?*        25

**Two**—Pain: The Body Breaks        33

*Have You Considered:*
*Why Does God Allow Christians to Suffer?*        41

**Three**—Abuse: When the Wolves Tear into the Sheep        47

*Have You Considered:*
*Why Would God Let This Happen to Me?*        59

**Four**—Addiction: A Dangerous Friend        69

*Have You Considered:*
*Why Is This Happening to My Loved One?*        81

**Five**—Shame: Run and Hide        87

*Have You Considered:*
*Where Is God When I'm Suffering?*        101

**Six**—Loneliness: Drowning in Depression        113

*Have You Considered:*
*How Do We Endure Through the Dark of Depression?*        125

**Seven**—Death: A Wolf Returns     133

*Have You Considered:*
*Why Does God Continue to Let Satan Have His Way?*    149


**Eight**—Anger: Damned Justice     159

*Have You Considered:*
*The Real Reason We Struggle with Anger?*    171


**Nine**—Judgment: Satan's Great Divider     177

*Have You Considered:*
*Why Do People Gossip and Spread Such Hurtful Words?*    195


**Ten**—Obedience: When God Demands Everything     199

*Have You Considered:*
*Embracing God's Purpose When You Are Suffering?*    209


**Eleven**—Doubt: Things Fall Apart     217

*Have You Considered:*
*What the Devil Means for Evil, God Can Turn for Good?*    229


**Twelve**—Humiliation: A New Wolf Appears     235

*Have You Considered:*
*How Gratitude Can Ease Our Worst Sufferings?*    243


**Thirteen**—The Lord Is Near to You     251

**Fourteen**—My Prayer for You     257

*Dear Reader*     262

*Dear Leader*     264

# *Dedication*

Jesus Christ shares a wonderful and profound invitation in Matthew 11:28-30: "Come unto me, all ye that labour and are heavy laden, and I will give you rest. Take my yoke upon you, and learn of me; for I am meek and lowly in heart: and ye shall find rest unto your souls. For my yoke is easy, and my burden is light."

Many years ago I heeded Jesus' offer and came unto Him. My heart often has been heavy laded, and I continually seek His rest. In my quest to learn of Christ, one matter I have come to deeply appreciate is the significance of cherishing forgiveness. As I have experienced God's unwavering forgiveness, I, too, choose to extend forgiveness to those who have caused me pain.

With immense gratitude, this book is dedicated to all the individuals whom God has guided me to forgive, allowing me to embark on a transformative journey with Christ Jesus.

## PSALM 77:1-3

I cried unto God with my voice, even unto God with my voice; and he gave ear unto me. In the day of my trouble I sought the Lord: my sore ran in the night, and ceased not: my soul refused to be comforted. I remembered God, and was troubled: I complained, and my spirit was overwhelmed. Selah.

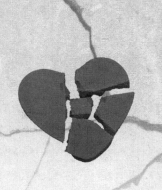

*Introduction*

# Where Is God
# When I Am Suffering?

IS GOD A GOOD GOD? Is my suffering a sign of His love or His hate? Why are awful things happening to me or to those I love?

If you're like me, you've asked these questions or something much like them. Life has no shortage of ways to make us suffer. Physical pain. Mistreatment, slander, oppression, and shame. Despair and death. The world can be a cruel place, whether you know Jesus as Lord or not.

Since 2013, my life has been extensively involved in ministry across the globe. I have seen the afflictions and suffering of countless people around the world. I have seen with my own eyes, heard with my ears, and touched with my hands many who are enduring various afflictions. Through these experiences, I have come to realize I am not alone in hardship. Suffering is common to everyone, yet many go through their anguish alone. They have no one to lift them up, listen to their sobs, and hug them compassionately.

Maybe this book will change that, at least a little bit. Perhaps my words can comfort you. It is my most desperate prayer they do. For I am not alone, and neither are you.

W HEN I WAS FIFTEEN, I gave my life to Christ Jesus. A better way to put it is that Jesus saved me.

It was a Saturday in February. Like most teenagers in the nineties, I sat in front of the television playing too much Nintendo and Sega with friends. Reading, on the other hand, held little appeal for me. Despite my determination to excel academically, I reluctantly delved into my schoolbooks and committed myself to studying.

However, when two dear friends, an elderly couple named Gene and Dottie Wittmeyer, purchased me my very own deluxe edition study Bible, I quickly developed a liking for reading it. I read it relentlessly; driven by a new hunger, desperation and eagerness to hear God's voice and figure out who He was in my life.

My life up to that point was a mixed bag. I was the son of two loving, fun, and devoted parents. But I was also the victim of foul sexual abuse, leading to a twisted sense of self and a body that was silently crying out for help. A persistent bedwetting habit closed me off from meaningful friendships, and my wonderful mother was struggling with addiction. To put it simply, I was overwhelmed and confused.

Thankfully I looked to Jesus for answers.

I was fascinated by how Christians spoke of God as if they knew Him personally. Growing up in a small church in Ohio where individuals were allowed to share their testimonies in the service, I always admired listening to the words of one particular man. He would get up, hold his Bible before the congregation, hug and kiss it, proclaiming his love for God and the Word. Then, he would always tell a story of how God touched his heart that week, leaving me in awe.

Around the same time, when I was twelve, my father got saved. He decided to surrender his sinful life and give himself to Christ. Quickly he purchased two new Bibles, one for himself and one for mother. From that day onward, he began reading the Scriptures and would discuss his daily learnings with us at home. My father, a high school dropout, had previously lived his life with no interest in God. However, when he was saved, many aspects of his life significantly changed overnight, including his newfound interest in the Bible. What amazed me was how much he understood from his readings.

At the age of twelve, I made a decision to read one chapter of the Bible every day and complete the whole book. Three years later, I still was reading the Bible, a chapter a day. And one day, my reading took me to Ephesians, the letter from the Apostle Paul that contains many powerful and memorable explanations of the gospel. I reached Chapter 2 and read these verses: "For by grace are ye saved through faith; and that not of yourselves: it is the gift of God: Not of works, lest any man should boast" (verses 8-9).

I couldn't help but read this passage several times. It leaped off the page and jolted me into a gripping sense of clarity about God, Heaven, Hell, salvation, and where I fit into everything.

The gospel tells a simple and beautiful story: God became a man and walked among us, focused all the while on the impending cross. Jesus Christ sacrificed Himself, allowing His perfect righteousness to be nailed to the cruel tree so the penalty for our sins would be paid in full.

Yet His death was not the end. Through His resurrection, Christ opened the gates to eternal life and sanctification here on Earth, which is why He is the way, the truth, and the life: Everything good flows through His existence, and in Him, we find all strength and provision. Regardless of our past sins and present weaknesses, Jesus' redemption can save us and give us a fresh start.

But that "fresh start" didn't make complete sense to me, and it may not be to you, either. If God was so loving, generous, and gracious to give His only Son for my sins, why had I suffered such wicked abuse? Why had it been allowed to endure for so long? And why had God allowed it to forever change me, twist and distort my identity?

It didn't make sense. I couldn't reconcile the God I'd learned about at church, and God I was reading about in Ephesians. What was it God was saving me from? What were the benefits of a life serving Him?

Did becoming a Christian give me special protection, like a force field against the evil of the world?

Coming to faith in Christ was the beginning of a long journey of wrestling with suffering. Whether or not you know Jesus as your personal Lord and Saviour, I imagine you are struggling with many of the same questions. On the surface, it doesn't make sense that Christ's followers would suffer such terrible illnesses and injustices. It doesn't seem right that Christians get cancer, fall victim to abuse, go to prison, become ensnared in addiction, or die tragic, premature deaths. Why would God allow that to happen anyway?

Yet the Scriptures are clear: God is good. God is love, and He is wise. He is also willing to put Himself on the line, sacrificing His own Son's flesh and blood to save sinners.

Who is this God? What is His nature, and how does our suffering factor into it?

If you're like me, you've been on a journey to understand God's character for some time. It's a deep quest, an expedition into the human heart and God's Word. It doesn't lead to easy answers, either. But it does lead to stunning beauty clothed in eternal purpose.

That purpose has everything to do with the life and person of Jesus Christ, the God-Man who lived, died, and rose again to reconcile sinners to the Father. He didn't live a life of abundant wealth and extravagant comfort. Rather, He walked humbly among us, befriending sinners and healing the sick, crippled, and demon-possessed. He spoke softly to sinners and showed them endless love.

Then He willingly paid the price for our sins on the cross before rising again to reconcile us to the Father.

Only by leaning into Jesus' life can we find peace with our suffering. Only by listening to Him, walking with Him, and trusting Him can any of it make sense. Getting there won't be easy, but it will absolutely be worth it.

I hope you'll join me on this quest. I hope you'll ask the difficult questions and struggle with the shocking answers.

Most importantly, I hope you find it in yourself to trust God with your suffering, to depend on Him for your provision, and to believe you are loved by the Creator of the universe, no matter what.

It's not an easy journey.

But it's worth it.

**ISAIAH 43:4**

Since thou wast precious in my sight, thou hast been honourable, and I have loved thee: therefore will I give men for thee, and people for thy life.

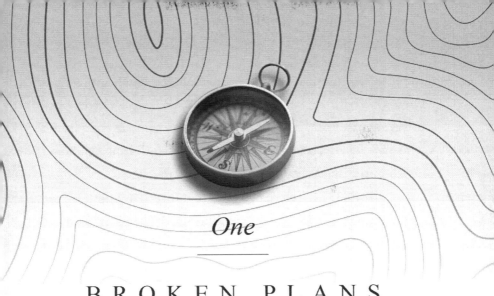

*One*

# BROKEN PLANS
## God's Clever Trick

OVER A DECADE AGO, GOD TRICKED ME into ministry work. Leading up to then, I was a successful small business owner, living a life of material comfort in beautiful, sunny San Diego. I had everything a modern American could want. A nice southern California home. A new car. Busy social life. Vacations around the world. And the ability to buy just about anything my heart desired.

Then God began deeply working in my heart.

It started as a mission trip to Mexico that I would share with four friends. However, by the time the plane left the ground, I was the only member of our party destined for an incredible time of serving abused and needy children in Latin America.

To that, I now say, God be praised!

God knew I needed a lot of help, much more than I imagined for myself. So the Lord devised a clever way to bring me to the hundreds, if not thousands, of people who would become my counselors—children, teachers, missionaries, and survivors of deep pain.

In 2013 I was a church-attending Christian. I was involved in a couple ministries within the church, such as prison ministry and street evangelism, and the Spirit had put a hunger in me to know and understand more of God. I desired for my life to be meaningful and significant somehow, but what I thought that meant was not what God had in mind.

In early July of that summer, four friends shared their plans to travel to Mexico for two weeks. They were putting together a trip to volunteer at an orphanage in Guadalajara. When I heard about their plans, something in my spirit leaped at the thought, and I wanted to join them. Right away, they included me in their plans.

Over the next several months, however, one by one, each had to drop out of the scheduled trip for October. By the time September came, it was only my friend Carol and myself. But Carol's schedule got mixed up, and she had to change her dates to two weeks earlier. By the time October arrived, it was only me boarding an airplane to Guadalajara.

After an enjoyable flight and smooth landing, I made it through the checkpoints and walked outside to the greeting area. An older gentleman was waiting for me with a paper in his hand that read my name. A polite smile was affixed to his face.

We greeted each other, and he walked me to the

other side of the parking lot where his van was parked. He had a humble demeanor, and was soft-spoken. His name was Robert Murillo, and he and his wife Joy had been missionaries in Mexico for decades. God had used them to establish a wonderful children's home for the many orphans in the region.

When we got into his van and he started to drive, he asked me a simple question: "So, what brings you down to Mexico with us?"

I honestly had no clue, and that's what I told him. "Brother," I said, "I don't know why I am here. I just want to serve and be a help to you in whatever way I can."

For the next two weeks, he took me up on those words. Missionary Murillo put me to work with many of the children's ministries and the church. He had me go out on the streets with some of his church members to evangelize and serve needy families. He had me teach the daily chapel at the school in the mornings. He had me work on the land with the children, milking cows, weeding and tending gardens, and much more. It was a busy but wonderful time.

What I enjoyed the most was getting to talk with the youngsters. Most kids open up more quickly than adults. Some of the kids shared their stories with me about how they ended up at the children's home. I couldn't believe what they revealed. The tribulations, abuse, and abandonment many of them had faced at such a young age were gut-wrenching. Some of them had been rescued from sexual abuse. Others had been freed from hunger and isolation.

One particular eight-year-old was so sweet. He had been at the orphanage for about a year. He was just starting to make basic sounds for language. Before being at the children's home, he had spent the better part of his life chained to a bed. His parents would get drunk, and his dad thought it was fun to burn his son with the end of cigarette buds to stub it out. Now, somehow, the boy had a beautiful smile. He was free to run around and play with other kids, go to school, and bathe in all the love, attention, and affirmation of God and the home parents. Clearly, what Missionary Murillo and his wife were doing was the Lord's work.

After I left the children's home and returned to America, I couldn't stop thinking about the stories I had heard and the lives being changed by the gospel of Jesus Christ. At this time in my life, I had secrets and sins that I promised myself never to divulge to anyone. But for the first time, I met people who could empathize with me and much more.

This was the very beginning of God patiently chiseling at my thick shell. God desired to work healing within me. Even more glorious, God desired to heal other people and invite me into their healing process all around the world. This is how my life in ministry around the world began.

Since 2013, God has slowly opened one opportunity after another for me to serve children, youth, and young adults all around the world. I have been invited to serve at many children's homes. I have had the honor of speaking at schools in various nations about sexual exploitation, abuse, and other relevant topics regarding the welfare of children. I have even had the opportunity to sit down one-on-one with politicians in several countries and talk to them about important children's rights.

But the greatest labor God has given me is to speak before churches and public squares about the Lord Jesus Christ and the abundant grace He gives to outcasts. For we are all outcasts whom God is calling to salvation.

Through these years of speaking publicly and meeting one-on-one with thousands of youngsters, God has used this ministry to help them as well as me. For I am needy and in need of His love and care. I used to think God gave ministry to someone to minister to others.

I was wrong.

I now understand God places people in ministry to minister to that individual. Once, someone said to me, "Lawrence, your ministry is great. These children really need you." I cringed within my spirit and softly replied, "Yes, these children need me, but I *need* these children much more."

This is the extraordinary miracle of service in Christ: It reorients our lives away from ourselves and toward others.

It also softens us, allowing us to be more vulnerable than we ever thought possible.

More than a decade of work in this precious arena has cracked my thick shell little by little. This has forced me to open up about my past secrets, hidden pains, and spiritual needs. For example, once in the Philippines, I was invited by a school principal to meet privately with a group of ten students who had experienced abuse. I agreed to talk with them. As I sat in that room, the principal introduced me to them by saying, "This is Brother Lawrence. He's a missionary, and he too was abused and is here to help you." I sat there thinking, "What am I going to say?" I felt the urge to open up and tell them everything, but I was afraid because I had never plainly told my story to anyone.

Yet the Spirit of Jesus Christ gave me strength, and for the first time, I openly shared with them the whole story of my trauma. I told them about my sexual abuse. I explained to them I felt lonely and disconnected from others many times. I even shared how sometimes I have had suicidal thoughts. Then I explained how God has been helping me. I told them I read and think about Jesus Christ daily by studying His Bible and communing with Him in prayer. It helps me so much.

At first, I was terribly anxious about how they would respond. Would they judge me or blame me for what happened? Would they scoff and tease me about my fears?

Yet what happened next was a fantastic miracle of God: The fear immediately melted off their faces. My transparency opened their hearts to talk to me and ask questions that had been in their hearts for a long time. We had a meaningful time together. Not only did they walk away encouraged, but I think I was even more encouraged than they were.

Time after time, God has lured me into unsettling decisions that I have been confronted with making. Would I open up and tell more people about my abuse or not? With guidance and dependence on God, I gradually became comfortable letting people hear my stories. However, I only told people outside the United States for a time. I thought, perhaps, I'll just help abroad and keep my past a secret from Americans.

God thought otherwise.

The word got out in the United States, and soon I began receiving confidential phone calls from others who had suffered horrific abuse, asking me to listen to their stories. I sympathetically listened to each individual's pains over the phone, and then I would share a little of my story. Little by little, God continued working on my hard heart, softening it up, and helping me be *real* and transparent with everyone.

Back in 2013, I would have found it hard to believe if someone had told me that, eventually, I would write a book in which I reveal my deepest nightmares, pains, insecurities, and secrets. I was convinced I would carry certain aspects of my life to the grave, keeping them known only to myself.

But God! How good and gracious our Lord is, with plans that clearly surpass our own. Hallelujah! In His infinite wisdom, He guides us on paths we may not comprehend, yet we should trust in His remarkable plan.

So here are some of my stories—a testament to God—who has given me a remarkable journey that has included many profound moments of suffering, pains, and afflictions to my mind, soul, and body. The following stories are a testament to which God allows hardships in this fallen, sinful world. This is because through His grace we are given the opportunity to learn valuable treasures of God otherwise we would never have known before.

I hope my words bring you comfort, help, and healing on your journey.

PHILIPPIANS 1:29

For unto you it is given in the behalf of Christ, not only to believe on him, but also to suffer for his sake;

*Have You Considered*

# Why Do I Still Suffer and Sin after Accepting Christ?

WHAT DID YOU EXPECT of the Christian life? Did you hope it would be easier, more comfortable, and free from temptation?

When we invite Christ into our hearts, it seems like a promise is made: Your life is going to be different now.

But what does "different" mean?

If you're like me, a part of you may have taken this to mean that life would be easier, comfortable, and sinless. Upon receiving Christ, it is natural to think our lives will be different from those of the non-believing world, specifically because we will be spared many of the worldly punishments God uses to show sinners the error of their ways. In other words, since I was in Christ, I thought I wouldn't suffer the slings and arrows of outrageous fortune anymore.

Yet so many of us find these slings and arrows abound post-salvation. In fact, they seem to multiply.

How can this be?

It is this question, this fundamental problem of life, that drove me to write this book. It is the question I am committed to exploring and hopefully unpacking in a way that reveals our hope.

The short of it is simple but not easily digestible: Our expectations were flawed. Mine certainly were.

I thought "different" meant "easier". But it didn't, and now I've come to believe it was never meant to be.

I think modern Christians believe their lives will be easier due to materialism, consumerism, false "prosperity" gospels, and our culture's dreams. The idea that salvation makes life "easier" is based on a massive lie that shall take us a lifetime to process. Many of us got into the faith thinking God wants our lives to be comfortable. The truth couldn't be more different, yet somehow it is wonderful and good!

Much to my surprise, God has frequently thrown my comfort and ease aside to support His heavenly purposes. With remarkable regularity and staggering efficiency, the Lord frustrates my worldly ambitions in order to draw me closer to Him.

Why would He do this? And if He does this kind of thing, how in the world is He good?

One of the earliest and most influential Christians, the Apostle Paul, experienced significant suffering in his life. When writing to the Corinthians about a nagging physical pain he was experiencing, Paul wrote that God refused to take the pain away. Instead, "...he said unto me, My grace is sufficient for thee: for my strength is made perfect in weakness. Most gladly therefore will I rather glory in my infirmities, that the power of Christ may rest upon me" (2 Corinthians 12:9).

Not only did Paul experience constant discomfort, he also prayed to God to take it away, and *God said "No."* Rather, God said something much more loving and eloquent, that His strength would be Paul's strength. But how would Paul access that strength? Through his own weakness.

This is entirely contrary to how human culture perceives strength, weakness, comfort, and pain. The atmospheric pressure of the world convinces us that our lives should be free of pain once we accept Christ into our hearts. However, this is not the case, nor was it ever *intended* to be the case.

This is true of sin, too. When we accept Jesus as Lord, we are tempted to believe we should cease to sin. In essence, this is true—we *should* sin no more—but it is untrue for everyone who has ever lived, except Christ, of course. "For all have sinned, and come short of the glory of God" Paul wrote in Romans 3:23. This is true prior to salvation and after, much to our regret.

Paul was equally forthcoming regarding sin and his post-salvific struggle with it, writing: "For that which I do I allow not: for what I would, that do I not; but what I hate, that do I. If then I do that which I would not, I consent unto the law that it is good. Now then it is no more I that do it, but sin that dwelleth in me. For I know that in me (that is, in my flesh,) dwelleth no good thing: for to will is present with me; but how to perform that which is good I find not. For the good that I would I do not: but the evil which I would not, that I do. Now if I do that I would not, it is no more I that do it, but sin that dwelleth in me" (Romans 7:15-20).

In brief, the man responsible for more than half of the books in the New Testament struggled with sin and suffering throughout his life, including after accepting Jesus as his Saviour. He knew sin was wrong and loathed it, yet he continued to succumb to it from time to time. As all believers should be, Paul was repentant, turning from it over and over. But to believe that Paul, or any other Christian, no longer strays from the *way* is a fallacy. All have sinned, and all continue to sin.

In theory, this makes complete sense. "Of course, he sinned," we might say. But we are often quick to make excuses, holding ourselves or one another to impossible standards. "Life was hard in those times," we may say of Paul and his time. "We have it much easier."

This, too, is false. What is it about our society that leads us to think we have it "easy"? Sure, from a worldly point of view, this is true.

From a biblical perspective, our "ease" can sometimes be a curse. In a way, modern conveniences just make it easier to sin. Thanks to mass marketing and screens, access to material goods has never been easier. Physical comforts like air conditioning and modern medicine ease discomfort and pain like never before. Some of these comforts have arguably numbed our ability to see our sin and depend on Jesus for our literal "daily bread".

These comforts are not enjoyed worldwide, either. With them or without them, life continues to be difficult. In the United States alone, 170 million people suffer loneliness, 21 million adults battle depression, and there is a widespread increase in self-harm and self-murder each year, which has deeply affected me and my family. This world sits under the shadow of a curse, a hateful corrupting influence that opposes God and all He stands for.

This is perhaps one of the most significant learning curves for believers in Christ to overcome: God desires our dependence, not our comfort. To the embattled sufferer, this may not come as a relief. How can God be loving when He doesn't make my pain go away?

Many of Christ's followers will testify their pain has brought them *closer* to God. They don't see God as the cause of the pain or even a cruel doctor guilty of malpractice by ignoring it. They see the pain as a reminder that the world is sinfully cursed and temporary, far from the deep satisfaction and fulfillment that comes from union with Christ.

They remember, too, our Saviour's profound sufferings. They remember that when He was in the Garden of Gethsemane and on the cross, Christ cried out in pain but received no relief. His pain was necessary to conquer death and open the tomb on Resurrection Sunday. This is explained when the author of Hebrews, believed by many to again be the Apostle Paul, wrote, "For we have not an high priest which cannot be touched with the feeling of our infirmities; but was in all points tempted like as we are, yet without sin" (Hebrews 4:15). Jesus Christ—God Himself—*knows* what it's like to suffer. He has been through more than we can imagine.

So why did He do it? To guilt us for our failures or mock us for our weaknesses?

Hardly.

Once more, the author of Hebrews offered profound comfort with these words: "Looking unto Jesus, the author and finisher of our faith; who for the joy that was set before him endured the cross, despising the shame, and is set down at the right hand of the throne of God" (Hebrews 12:2).

Jesus chose to endure the cross because it overjoyed Him and His Father and Spirit to win us back to God. He did it out of love. Pure, perfect, sacrificial love.

The purpose of life isn't to avoid suffering or achieve perfect righteousness on our own.

The purpose of our lives is to be fully dependent on God, leaning with complete trust in Jesus' ability to comfort us in pain and sanctify us from sin.

This is not what the world sold us when we accepted Jesus into our hearts. But it is the good and glorious path Jesus promised in His Word through His Holy Spirit.

If you are still suffering—or if you are still contending with habitual sin—take heart, for Jesus is with you, and you are right where He wants you to be.

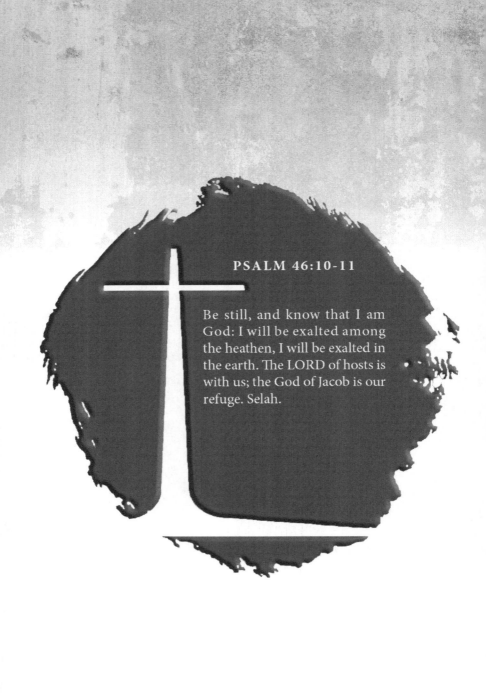

**PSALM 46:10-11**

Be still, and know that I am God: I will be exalted among the heathen, I will be exalted in the earth. The LORD of hosts is with us; the God of Jacob is our refuge. Selah.

## *Two*

---

# PAIN
# The Body Breaks

ONE MINUTE I'M SLEEPING peacefully in my bed. The next, I'm twisting and screaming.

I awake suddenly to the sensation of someone stabbing me in the lower lumbar with a hot knife. My back is spasming, and there's almost nothing I can do to stop it.

"Oh, God!" I cry to Heaven. "Please heal me!"

I painfully and slowly lift myself out of bed, hoping to alleviate the pain. I force myself out of bed and walk into the other room. I fall down onto the floor next to the couch and scream, "Ahhh! Oh God, help me!"

I am stuck on the floor. Agony shoots down from my lower lumbar to my feet like someone is ripping and tearing the muscles.

My back seizes and spasms again.

"Ahhh! God! Why so much pain?"

I wriggle until I'm on my side, where I can steal a pinch of comfort. But after a minute, the sharp pains rockets down my legs, hips, and back again. One leg leans over such that my lower back twists a little too far, erupting in unspeakable pain. "Please God, stop the pain!"

I need to flatten myself out. This position is making it so much more painful, stretching the muscles to the point of breaking—

*I can't move.*

My leg feels paralyzed by the pain. I can't move it because the muscles are locked in place and seizing nonstop. I gasp for breath, the sensation like a thousand knives piercing my flesh.

"God... help me..."

I need to flip over. To somehow get out of this awkward position and make the agony stop. I reach above me, hoping to grab something for leverage. My couch has a bunch of pillows, and I swipe at them, knocking some off the couch and trying to lift myself up. What am I supposed to hold onto?

The movement tweaks my back muscles, and I yelp, more blades digging into my flesh and twisting their cruel edges. I press my hands against the wall. I have to do something, *anything* to get out of this pain.

Then my fingers grasp the arm of the couch. It's hardly a good hold, but it'll have to do. I grab it as tightly as I can and push.

The tearing sensation rushes up my body like a wave, and I wonder if my inwards are anything more than shredded paper. My legs slowly rotate until they slide onto the couch, parallel to one another. I collapse and suck air as if I've just finished a marathon.

"Oh God," I moan between sips of air. "Pleassse God... don't let that happen again."

It would happen again. Night and day for two months. My world was a den of relentless pain and sleepless hours on a sweat-stained bed.

I couldn't work. I couldn't minister. I couldn't move around.

My world was in pain, and my body was crumbling.

How could God let this happen to me? Didn't He want me to do His good work in ministry?

Or had He abandoned me to suffer forever?

BACK PAIN SEEMS to run in my family. My mother has had back and body troubles since I was a little boy. She lives in constant pain, and years ago struggled with an addiction to painkillers. My older brother John has suffered his own back troubles too.

As for me, I was diagnosed with a minor scoliosis condition in my early twenties. Since then, I have always tried to sit straight and maintain a proper posture. To supplement this, I have for years maintained the discipline to work out and build strong core muscles so my back will have adequate support. I have even made a conscious decision to sleep on the floor every night for years to encourage proper alignment of my back.

Despite my efforts to stay fit and sleep on the floor, my back troubles have caused me some problems over the years. It could be much worse, but there are still moments when the back decides to lock up for several days and puts me on the floor. It's happened in public, alone in the shower, in all kinds of places. My muscles have cramped so severely two or three times that I truly believed I would suffocate to death. My body has added sciatica nerve pain around my lower left back, hips, and legs to worsen the suffering. By stretching, I've been able to manage the pain, which has been a significant relief.

But stretching doesn't always work.

In 2021, I moved to El Salvador to minister to young people involved with the MS-13 and Calle 18 gangs. Salvadorans love soccer, and while I had previously only played soccer three times in my entire life, I figured I should learn to play so I could fellowship with the youth more. Our Salvadoran church had even started a soccer ministry with teens and young guys in our neighborhood, meeting once a week so we could interact with men who desperately needed Christ. However, the field we took them to wasn't quite a "field". It was a court paved with cement.

There I learned to play on that hard-topped soccer court and enjoyed the game quite a bit. However, the locals didn't take it easy on me just because I was new. I regularly tumbled on the concrete during each match. While it hurt, I was overjoyed to be a part of this community. I loved it!

But all that falling took its toll on my body. The bruises and beatings accumulated so that I woke up in severe pain later in the year. The nerves down my left leg, hip, and lower lumbar were killing me! I could barely get off the floor. Stretches provided some relief, but most of the time, they didn't help at all. I gritted my teeth and forced myself to walk to continue participating in the ministry. The pain lasted four months; finally, it was gone entirely by late spring of the following year.

I tried to hide the pain during this time, but people knew it was there. I attended church services but often found it difficult to sit for more than ten minutes. The plastic chairs were terribly uncomfortable, so I would stand in the back. When it was time for me to teach Sunday School, I had to use extra notes to keep my mind on track of what I wanted to say. It became a recurring joke that Lawrence was aging faster than anyone else, and now he was a crippled old man. They called me Mr. "Anciano" or "Old Man".

The pain finally abated for a season. However, in late November 2022, it resurfaced, albeit mildly. Then on January 5, 2023, it returned worse than ever. It was excruciating torment, suffering sent straight from hell. My lower lumbar and buttocks felt like someone was stabbing me over and over with a sharp chef's knife. Both my legs felt like someone was stretching and tearing them apart. My hips trembled as if they were shattered into thousands of pieces. Walking was a nightmare because I could barely stand for a full minute.

Over two months, it was torture beyond imagination. I struggled to get out of bed and didn't leave home unless it was essential. All the ministry I was accustomed to doing was unavailable. When I felt up to it, I would call individuals to talk and encourage them. However, the pain was so awful that for many days I succumbed to only focusing on myself.

This is perhaps the great evil of physical pain: It reveals how selfish we are. It urges us to retreat inward, put up defenses, and focus on our own survival above all else.

I get it: I didn't want to do anything for anyone when my sciatica pain flared. I could barely stand up or walk. All I could do was lay on my bed for hours, crying, sometimes yelling out to God. Thinking about sharing the gospel with others barely registered in my mind. All I could focus on was finding a solution to my agony.

What are we supposed to do when suffering physical pain? Should we do our best to ignore the agony and carry on as if everything is fine? Can we allow ourselves time to heal without worrying about duty and responsibility?

Or is the answer something in between, something much more Christlike and holy than we can imagine on our own?

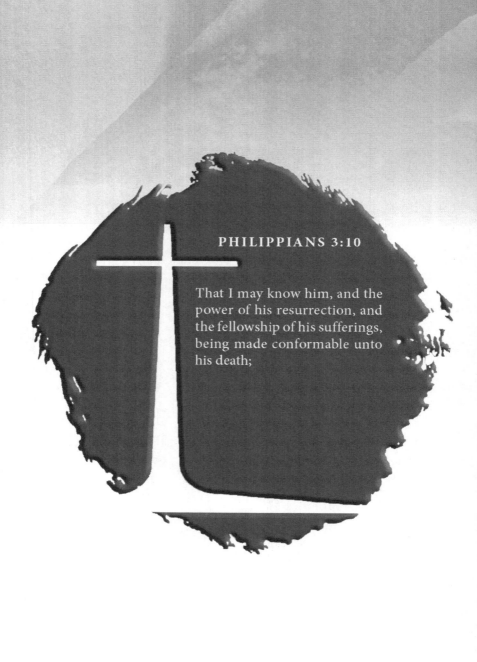

**PHILIPPIANS 3:10**

That I may know him, and the power of his resurrection, and the fellowship of his sufferings, being made conformable unto his death;

## *Have You Considered*

---

# Why Does God Allow Christians to Suffer?

HAVE YOU EVER SUFFERED SEVERE PAIN? Has God ever thrown you a curveball and completely upended your plans?

Perhaps you've been in my shoes. Your pain might be worse, and for that, you have my sincerest and most deepest compassion. Your pain is your own, and no one can tell you how easy you do or do not have it.

We can all agree physical pain is terrible. While our pain is unique to our own experiences, physical discomfort is familiar to all human beings, including Christ's followers. Calling Jesus our Lord offers many blessings in this life; however, it doesn't exempt us from diseases and disorders like sciatica, diabetes, or rare forms of cancer. We are all under the curse of this fallen world.

Yet there is hope for those of us whose bodies are breaking or broken; that hope is in the life of the Lord Jesus Christ.

It is written of God's servant, the Messiah, who would come to save humanity from its sins: "He is despised and rejected of men; a man of sorrows, and acquainted with grief: and we hid as it were our faces from him; he was despised, and we esteemed him not. Surely he hath borne our griefs, and carried our sorrows: *yet we did esteem him stricken, smitten of God, and afflicted.* But he was wounded for our transgressions, he was bruised for our iniquities: the chastisement of our peace was upon him; and with his stripes we are healed" (Isaiah 53:3-5, emphasis added).

When God chose to become a man, a holy and blameless man who would lead His people to salvation, He did not choose a life of painless bliss. He did not shield Himself from the evils of the world. In fact, He regularly subjected Himself to those evils, enduring hunger, thirst, exhaustion, pain, and even death. Jesus "carried our sorrows." He was "wounded for our transgressions" and "bruised for our iniquities." He did nothing wrong, nothing to deserve suffering, yet He suffered more than any person who has ever lived.

This isn't how I viewed Christ when I was suffering. I viewed Him not as a fellow sufferer but as a inattentive father for not healing me. For those months of sciatica affliction, I sometimes found myself getting angry at God. I would lie on the floor and cry, begging for help. My prayers cried so hard and I felt unbelievably lonely. Even worst of all, I sometimes felt like God was judging me, punishing me for my sins because I somehow hadn't repented of them hard enough.

The majority of my prayers during this season were far from sweet, either. Instead of offering praise and seeking Him for increased faith and patience, I foolishly yelled at Him. I hurled accusations His way, alleging that He hadn't lived up to the expectations I held. In my misguided moments, I questioned His goodness.

*Well,* you might think, *maybe if God was actually good, He would have healed you.*

I hear that, and I have to call it what it is: A lie from Satan.

God's goodness doesn't depend on my physical comfort or pain. It has everything to do with His character, revealed through His sanctifying power, made available through Christ's atoning sacrifice on the cross. My earthly pain is a byproduct of living in a fallen, evil world, a haven for devilish powers. Satan corrupts and lies; he doesn't create. His work is to take something good, like my body, twist it and befoul it for his own broken intentions.

Yet God through Jesus' humble life, shows us life is about so much more than physical comfort. Life is about trusting the Father. Life is about leaning on God for everything.

If I only trust God when my body is completely comfortable, what kind of testimony is that? And if I only believe God can heal when He specifically heals me, what kind of witness is that?

We are quick to put a premium on our own lived experiences. Thanks to the Enlightenment philosophy and postmodernism, truth is sold as a relative, personal creation. And while there are some examples of "lived truth," there is only one absolute truth—the truth of Jesus Christ. And the truth is that God is good and God is love, no matter what Satan does to convince us otherwise.

Physical suffering reveals who we really are and what we really believe will save us. It strips away our ability to pick ourselves up and reminds us that we are mortal beings with limited time on this dusty planet. When youth and strength fail; when health succumbs to illness; when all else fades, in what then will we hope?

Physical pain can be seen as a gift, as it serves to remind us of our inherent truth: our weaknesses and sins, our dependence and neediness. We truly *need* God; pain emphasizes that our only hope lies in the promise of eternal life through Jesus Christ. Similarly, Jesus rejected the fleeting promises of this world in favor of an everlasting hope.

I have no idea how severe your pain is. I can neither comprehend nor appreciate how difficult it has made your life. I haven't been there with you in the long, agonizing hours as you struggle to keep your sanity while your body screams and revolts against what is happening. I can't possibly know the extent of your suffering.

However, I do know you are not alone in suffering. I know you have a friend in the man of sorrows, the one acquainted with grief. You have a God who has lived through what you are going through, all so He could win you over to Himself for all time. This may not ease the pain, but it can give the pain purpose. It can somehow make the horror of agony a beautiful opportunity.

Jesus wants you to experience intimate closeness with Him that extends beyond this physical world. Yes, physical pain is a curse, an unspeakable misery we all must endure. But we don't have to endure it alone. We have a humble Saviour-servant friend who washed His disciples' dirty feet, endured a best friend's betrayal, and took savage beatings and nails through his flesh to unite us with the Father.

Jesus is with you. He is near to you. He has been through it and wants to be with you every step of the way. Try not to get mad at Him when you are going through anguish. Instead, sit before God in silence and listen to His Spirit. Talk to Him. Invite Him into your suffering. Ask Him to suffer with you. To be your friend and encourager. To give the pain a purpose.

Christ wants to hug you with grace, and He desires you to be near Him in the midst of suffering. Then you will be one step closer to achieving that precious promise of faith: peace that passes all human understanding.

The peace of God.

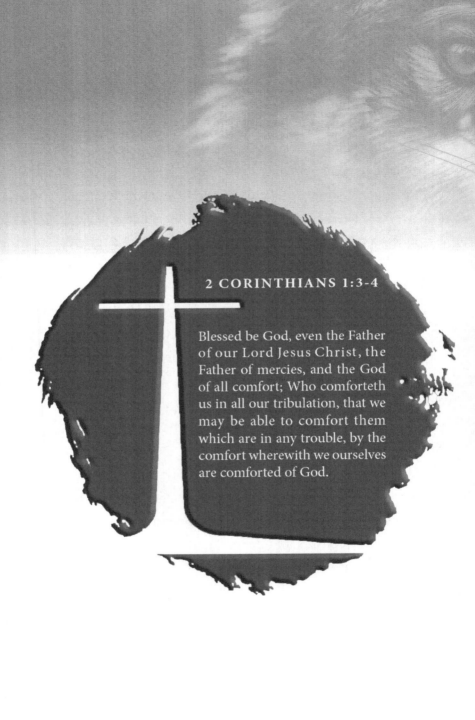

## 2 CORINTHIANS 1:3-4

Blessed be God, even the Father of our Lord Jesus Christ, the Father of mercies, and the God of all comfort; Who comforteth us in all our tribulation, that we may be able to comfort them which are in any trouble, by the comfort wherewith we ourselves are comforted of God.

## *Three*

---

# A B U S E
# When the Wolves Tear into the Sheep

THIS ISN'T EASY TO TALK ABOUT. It probably won't be easy to read, either.

Nevertheless, I'm convinced if we don't reckon with Satan's corrupting influence, we can't truly depend on Jesus and trust Him as fully as we should.

When I was a young child, no older than seven or eight, I was sexually abused by a trusted uncle. Although my parents taught me I should protect myself, as most parents do, my family member was clever in his betrayal when they weren't around.

Before I go any further, I think it's important to pause and consider an important question.

Why should I talk about this at all? Why give Satan so much time in the spotlight? Why revel in the filth of a vile person?

The last thing I want to do is give Satan a moment more of my time and energy. But he has devoted his entire existence to destroying God's people and turning them away from the truth. We cannot engage in a holy battle with our fingers in our ears, trying to tune out the things we don't want to hear. Perhaps Satan knew all along I would become a warrior for the gospel later in life, so he threw his worst at me as a child. I won't know until I go Home to be with Jesus.

I talk about my abuse for two reasons.

First, I want to show how powerful God is in healing someone who went through what I did. I testify to His mercy and grace to lift me out of the pit, an ongoing process that will likely be for the rest of my life.

The second reason I share is because I am not alone. Abuse is a topic many of us don't like to hear about. It disrupts the comfortable status quo and forces us to gear up for battle against the forces of darkness.

But I am one of many. Even worse, many of my fellow victims are abused by loved ones and trusted adults who claim to be Christians. How evil it is that they mask their wickedness with the name of our wonderful Saviour!

We must summon the courage to hear these stories and empathize with those who suffer. We must come alongside our abused brothers and sisters and offer them welcoming hearts with hugs, genuine ears to listen to, and sincere times of fellowship. We must also rise up against those who shelter or protect abusers and cleanse the House of the Lord of this evil.

I promise to tell these stories with utmost care. The last thing I want to do is further the traumas I endured or put ideas in your mind that lead you to sin in whatever fashion the devil has crafted.

To start, I'll say this: My parents sought my and my siblings' safety and trained us for this. They imposed rules and curfews. They provided us with code words to prevent us from falling into the trap of abduction or harm. They taught us there were dangerous people out there.

And somehow, it happened anyway.

I REFUSE TO SAY HIS REAL NAME. I also don't want to give him a fictitious name. He is "my abuser," nothing more.

With that said, my abuser lived with us through several periods of my childhood. One of my earliest memories was him inviting me to sit on his lap.

I was a youngster at the time. I remember so little about the day and time, and location. I distinctly remember we were alone, and an adult I admired had invited me to be close to him. What kid wouldn't be delighted?

He asked me about the toy I was playing with and complimented me on how cool it was. I showed him how it worked, and he seemed genuinely interested in it and me.

Then he told me he had his own "secret" toy.

This just shows how insidious evil can be. My abuser used two familiar and healthy behaviors of a loving adult—

safe physical contact (lap-sitting) and creative play—to exploit my trust in him. He somehow circumvented whatever safeguards my parents taught me. I'm sure they could have done better to prepare me; I'm certain of it. The fact remains they tried and failed because my abuser was far craftier than they thought a pedophile would be.

Since he lived with us, my abuser had plenty of opportunities to interact and spend time alone with me. Our "game" with his "special toy" took many forms, and he trained me to believe I was being a good boy when we were together. This groomed me to see his behavior as good and usual. I felt important to my abuser. I felt secure and wanted in his presence.

Yet it was all a terrible lie, and it corrupted me at a very young age.

My abuser wasn't the only person to physically violate me, either. Several years later, between the ages of seven and eleven, a friend of my parents would put his hands on me during visits to our home. This person isn't worthy of naming, either, so we'll call him "the creep".

Even in a crowded room, my mother and father mere inches from us, the creep would reach toward the back of me and poke his fingers inside me. I was shocked! What in the world did this person think he was doing?

One time when he visited our home, I tried to escape his presence by going to another room. He quickly poked at my butt and grinned.

"Stop that," I said.

The creep towered over me and patted me on the back with a smile, as if everything was alright. "What's the matter, sissy?" he taunted, grinning as if I was the one in the wrong. "I thought you liked it."

"No, I don't!" I snapped.

He laughed at me and walked away as if nothing had happened.

That particular time he couldn't have his way; other times, I wasn't so lucky, and he'd successfully get his hands onto my butt and try to poke his fingers inside me.

Why was he doing this? I didn't act like a sissy. I definitely didn't act like I wanted him or anyone else to touch me like that. Was there something wrong with me?

After every encounter with that man, I was consumed with disgust, confusion, and frustration. I felt a particular vexation toward my parents, who often witnessed the motions he made but thought it was simple jostling. In hindsight, I should have called him out for his behavior. But what eight-year-old boy has the courage to do such a thing? I certainly didn't. No one would believe me. Worse, perhaps they'd blame and accuse me of being a little dirty boy. Of course, such a thought is absurd to think now, but then, as a young boy, I was terrified of what they'd think and then do to punish me.

Why did these men target me? Was it something particular about me? Or did I just happen to be the innocent lamb straying at the edge of the enclosure?

When we are the recipients of abuse, violence, or mistreatment, it is easy and natural to blame ourselves.

Worse, parts of our culture engage in victim-blaming as well. There are indeed some false accusers out there, but the vast majority of victims are telling the truth.

I didn't speak up about the truth for a long time. The shame was too much to bear. To make matters worse, my experiences had wired my brain to consider girls *and* boys attractive. By my early teen years, I was actively fantasizing about my female as well as male classmates. Everything that happened with my abuser taught me that overtly sexual behavior was completely normal. This was how guys built a special relationship. He completely warped my understanding of what a healthy, God-breathed relationship should look like.

Human sexuality is a beautiful creation, a gift from God that leads to incredible flourishing and pleasure. God designed it to reflect His glory, specifically as illustrated by Christ's loving sacrifice for the Church, His Bride. Yet these predators twisted this divine gift into a Frankenstein monster of lust, perversion, and humiliation. Like all abusers, they preyed on my innocence and warped my sense of self.

Worst of all, they didn't only hurt me in the midst of my protests. Instead, my abuser lured me to enjoy what he was doing. He conditioned me to believe his evil acts were healthy and fun.

I can't think of anything more Satanic than this: To take someone innocent and teach them that innocence is guilt and sin is pleasurable freedom. That's precisely what my abuser did, and I have been untangling his wicked lies ever since.

I T TOOK ME A LONG TIME to tell anyone about my abuse. At the age of 31, I finally shared my story with my mother; my father found out several years later. They were brutal conversations but necessary for me to begin the healing process, to reconcile the fact that they had unwittingly welcomed this monster into our home and entrusted him with my care. They had unknowingly turned a blind eye to years of warning signs that my abuser was up to something, and their boy was being groomed and molested under their noses.

Yet they weren't the ones who abused me. Their failure to protect me wasn't due to blatant sin or reckless leadership; it arose from a lack of awareness. They trusted my abuser and never thought he'd be like one of the perverts "out there" who were targeting little boys (just like "the creep" they considered to be a trusted friend).

Ultimately, I shared my story to heal, not to place blame. If we are to lay blame, it rests on Satan and the men who violated me.

But assigning blame is the easy part. It never brings healing. It may bring clarity, but never closure.

I needed to heal. I needed wholeness and peace, something I could only find in the arms of my loving Saviour.

So how am I healing from all of this?

I had been trying to heal for years but didn't know it. In the moments I've chosen to embrace my same-sex attraction, I thought it would soothe the pain I constantly felt due to my abuser's actions. It hasn't. Instead, it tore open old wounds and reinforced feelings of inadequacy, shame, and loneliness.

I tried to heal in other ways, too. I built a successful small business and accumulated the comforts of a thriving San Diego lifestyle. Yet all the while, I felt a constant sense of dissatisfaction. It was all meaningless. It was a shallow existence, and I knew it all along.

For years I ran from my trauma rather than confronting it head-on. A crucial aspect of understanding suffering is to realize that sometimes God allows us to seek comfort elsewhere so we can discover how empty and fruitless it truly is. This is essential knowledge for followers of Christ.

God allows us to suffer when we seek comfort outside of His presence.

When I ran to my same-sex attraction and entertained my fantasies, I came away with crushing loneliness and hurt anew. When I fled into worldly wealth, I felt nothing but discontentment.

Why would God allow such suffering?

Here is the brilliance of our Lord. He doesn't "punish" us for seeking comfort outside of ourselves. Rather, the punishment is self-evident. To seek worldly comfort itself *is the punishment.* God doesn't need to afflict us further.

Like the lost son who fled from his loving father in the Bible, we must often live out our fleshly longings to discover how foolish they truly are. Once we've exhausted these dreams, we come to our senses and hurry home.

And how does our Father greet us?

Let's read the story in the Bible: "But when [the son] was yet a great way off, his father saw him, and had compassion, and ran, and fell on his neck, and kissed him," Jesus explains. "And the son said unto him, Father, I have sinned against heaven, and in thy sight, and am no more worthy to be called thy son. But the Father said to his servants, Bring forth the best robe, and put it on him; and put a ring on his hand, and shoes on his feet: And bring hither the fatted calf, and kill it; and let us eat, and be merry: For this my son was dead, and is alive again; he was lost, and is found..." (Luke 15:20-24).

This is not how we tend to imagine God reacting to us when we come to Him in shame. I tend to imagine a furious, red-faced father who is ready to slap me or send me packing. For many of us, this is the picture of our own fathers and stepfathers, the men who set a poor example of God in our lives.

Yet Jesus tells of a loving father, a man swift in forgiveness and generosity. The father in the story not only accepts his son but runs to him, kisses him, and sacrifices more of his wealth to welcome the boy back to the family.

When the son first demanded his share of the inheritance, the father didn't refuse. Clearly, the son had made up his mind, and the father knew an argument wouldn't build trust or understanding. In the same way, God allows His children to have things their way, at least for a time. He allows us to indulge in our secular fantasies because He knows they'll fail to satisfy us fully. In this regard, suffering is absolutely necessary for our sanctification in becoming more like Christ.

What about the trauma I was trying to overcome? What about the evil perpetrators imposed upon me before I could defend myself or even understand what was happening?

Why would God ever allow *that* to happen?

In other words, if God is good, why would He allow my abuser and the creep to do such evil things to me, and for so long?

This is a terribly difficult question, and it nearly broke me.

But I've come to an answer, and it unlocks our ability to endure almost anything.

Why does God allow such awful things to happen?

Because God isn't in the business of preventing suffering. He never has been, despite what I may think. In fact, God lived a life on Earth just to prove it.

I am hardly the only survivor of this kind of abuse. I am one of many. Millions, in fact.

I've had the privilege of meeting some of these fellow survivors during my ministry. As I have traveled across the United States, over the ocean to Asia, and into the tropics of Latin America and Africa, I have met many young people who are similar to how I was. They are young, weary, and confused. Their heads hang, and their eyes struggle to rise to meet mine. Lies and secret twisted schemes beat them down. They are lost.

But then God brings me into their lives. God puts me in a situation where I get to sit with these young people, tell them my story, and watch their eyes widen at the truth: *They are not alone.*

I made it. I am enduring. God lifted me out of the pit and continues to heal the pain and trauma.

Now it's their turn. My journey of healing can become their journey, too. My hope becomes their hope. And as much as they need me, I need them just as much. They encourage me and help me each time we meet one another.

This is Christ's power in our world. Why do we suffer abuse? So we can learn to depend on God's unconditional love and pass that love on to others who desperately need it. As Paul wrote to the Corinthians in his second letter, "Blessed be God, even the Father of our Lord Jesus Christ, the Father of mercies, and the God of all comfort; Who comforteth us in all our tribulation, that we may be able to comfort them which are in any trouble, by the comfort wherewith we ourselves are comforted of God." (2 Corinthians 1:3-4).

Our God is a God of comfort, but to be comforted, we must suffer. We cannot know how good He is until we've been under Satan's thumb. God longs to love us and promises to do it, we simply need to accept Him and His unending love.

As we struggle with the suffering of abuse and bring it to Jesus, I hope you receive His unending love and trust Him with your pain. He is able to join you in that suffering, heal you, and comfort you.

I know He can do it because it's what He has done and is doing with me.

**2 CORINTHIANS 4:17**

For our light affliction, which is but for a moment, worketh for us a far more exceeding and eternal weight of glory;

*Have You Considered*

# Why Would God Let
# This Happen to Me?

THIS QUESTION HAS THE POWER to break people. "If there is a God and He is good, why would such a good God allow _____ to happen?" people ask. It's the kind of question people ask when they hold the existence of God in their hands.

I don't blame them. It's a question I've asked on countless occasions. So many people don't understand why our world is cursed with so much pain and so many atrocities. War, starvation, poverty, rape, drugs, and gangs: It's all too much to carry, and it can easily break our spirits if we let it.

We must resist by leaning into God's truth and His way. A passage that has comforted me in my search for answers originates in the writings of Isaiah, a prophet during the divided kingdom phase of Israel's history. "For my thoughts are not your thoughts," Isaiah transcribed for God, "neither are your ways my ways, saith the LORD. For as the heavens are higher than the earth, so are my ways higher than your ways, and my thoughts than your thoughts" (Isaiah 55:8-9).

As a young man, I read this text to mean, "I'm smarter than you, so trust me." But God speaks of so much more than mere knowledge. Biblical scholars and experts on the original Hebrew often translate "ways" to mean devising or planning. Since God is an entirely different being from mankind, we must assume His way of forming ideas and processes is distinct and alien from our own. His "ways," or processes, are nothing like ours.

This is why the life of Jesus is so significant and radical in biblical history. He breathes life into every self-description found in the Old Testament. He is the embodiment of God in human form.

The Apostle John wrote, "In the beginning was the Word, and the Word was with God, and the Word was God. The same was in the beginning with God. All things were made by him; and without him was not any thing made that was made. In him was life; and the life was the light of men. And the light shineth in darkness; and the darkness comprehended it not" (John 1:1-5).

Jesus is the embodiment of the Word of God spoken in the Old Testament; He is the incarnate flesh of God's "thoughts" and "ways" in living tissue. Jesus is God Himself in human form.

With this profound reality in mind, we must turn to

Jesus for a deeper comprehension of God and His ways. The world has corrupted our understanding of how life should be lived. We are children of darkness, and as the Apostle John wrote, the "darkness comprehended it not" (vs. 5). We simply don't get it. We can't unless God saves us and gives us eyes to see the Light for what it is.

That doesn't soothe our pain from this troublesome question, though, the question I asked over and over while I reeled from the havoc my abusers wrought upon me: "If there is a God and He is good, why would He allow _____ to happen?"

Jesus is the living person of God and His ways. We can assume what He did is what God does.

With that in mind, we need to confront some challenging questions:

Did Jesus lift His hand and stop every bad thing from happening during His time on Earth? Did He put an end to all hunger, war, violence, criminal activity, and corruption?

No. He did not.

In fact, He didn't even prevent these things from happening in the first place.

But wait! Didn't Jesus heal people and bring some back from the dead?

He sure did. But note the language here. He *healed* people. He didn't prevent them from suffering or dying in the first place.

Do you know what else Jesus didn't do? He didn't fix the political situation that had the Jews completely up in arms.

During His time walking the Earth, Israel wasn't an independent nation. Sure, it had kings of its own (the Herod dynasty) who made trouble for the people, but those kings were mere vassals to the true boss: Rome. The Roman Empire was at the peak of its global influence with territories spanning the Mediterranean, Europe, North Africa, and the Middle East. One of its regions was Palestine; it even installed a governor there whom you may have heard of: Pontius Pilate.

How did the Israelites feel about this? In a word: Indignant.

Rebellions were frequent, and the Romans mercilessly put them down. The perpetrators suffered torture and crucifixion for their crimes. Heavy taxes were levied on the subjects of Caesar, with Jews employed to do the dirty work of collecting the money. Matthew, who wrote the gospel that bears his name, was a tax collector himself. Another of Jesus' disciples, Simon the Zealot, abandoned his commitment to fighting the Romans to follow Christ.

For hundreds of years, the Hebrew people believed a Messiah was coming to destroy Israel's enemies. To them, this prophecy was purely geopolitical. Israel certainly had its reasons to hope for this. It had already suffered exile and captivity under several empires, including the Assyrians and Babylonians. Worse, they hadn't heard any word from God via a prophet for over four hundred years. Understandably, they wanted God to reenter the picture with a bang.

Expectations soared through the roof when Jesus

arrived, claiming to be the Messiah. But Jesus was not the Messiah they hoped for. Instead of leading a battle against the Romans, Jesus taught about the enemy within, *sin*. Instead of being crowned king of Israel by the people, He wore a crown of thorns before His executioners. Instead of praising the religious elite for their piety and righteousness, He rebuked them as hypocrites. Jesus was as countercultural as they come.

We have to admit something shocking about Jesus. He did little—perhaps even *nothing*—to prevent suffering during His time on earth. When He performed miracles, they offered healing from prior, long-existing suffering. Other miracles, such as feeding the 5,000+ and providing more wine at a wedding, offered delightful but brief respites from the material worries of this world.

Jesus didn't multiply Roman coins to help people get rich. Jesus didn't build houses or command His disciples to do so. Jesus didn't cure all diseases or put an end to all physical death. He refused to overthrow unjust political regimes and assume any earthly power for Himself.

He was tempted to do these things and refused each and every time. Who tempted Him by chance?

Satan himself.

"Then was Jesus led up of the Spirit into the wilderness to be tempted of the devil... the devil taketh him up into an exceeding high mountain, and sheweth him all the kingdoms of the world, and the glory of them; And saith unto him, All these things will I give thee, if thou wilt fall down and worship me. Then saith Jesus unto him, Get thee hence, Satan: for it is written, Thou shalt worship the Lord thy God, and him only shalt thou serve" (Matthew 4: 1, 8-10).

To put it simply, Jesus was tempted by a successful life. If you read the entirety of the scene, you'll see Jesus was tempted by three things:

- Food
- Safety
- Power

Jesus rejected all three, quoting His Father's word each time.

How this flies in the face of our expectations of God and a good life! How this contradicts our hopes and dreams, most of which are a product of the culture, not the gospel!

Jesus didn't come to end physical suffering. He eased it for a large number of people, providing a foretaste of what was to come.

But every aspect of His life was focused on one passionate element: The Cross. Jesus' mission was to pay the price for our sins—yours, mine, even my abuser's, should he repent and turn to the Lord—not to make our lives easier or more comfortable. And while injustice grieves Him immensely, Jesus' plan wasn't to stamp it out entirely during His life. He intends to put an end to all suffering, all injustice, and all evil when He returns and consummates His Kingdom.

But not yet.

This is the agony and splendor of the Kingdom

of Heaven as it is today. It is the "now and not yet," the presence of God's Kingdom today amidst the reign of terror from Satan. Eternal peace is here, yet it must survive the sadistic behavior of a man like my abuser.

As for my abuse, I have come to peace with it. God allowed it to happen, much like He permits all of Earth's evils to persist, for a singular purpose: to draw us close to Christ.

It may be difficult to admit, we often carry an inherent arrogance and self-reliance. We become consumed by the pursuit of security, success and pleasures through our own efforts, such as careers, finances, and the daily distractions of life, rather than leaning into fellowship with God and adhere to His Word for sustenance. Nonetheless, God's faithful love for us is unwavering, and He is with us, even in the darkest of times. Sometimes, God allows circumstances that we can't fully grasp in order to draw us closer to Him. He desires a deep, abiding relationship with us, one where we rely on His guidance and find strength in His Word. Thus He uses the harsh realities of this sinful world to reveal the hidden depths of our hearts, enabling us to see the sins hidden within us. He allows grief and pain so that can we recognize our spiritual distance from God.

While we may never completely understand all the reasons behind our suffering, we can find solace in knowing that God's ultimate purpose is to bring us closer to Him, to strengthen our faith, and to remind us that our true sustenance comes from our connection with Him. In this journey of life, our fellowship with God is of paramount importance, and

He walks with us through every tribulation, offering His love and support along the way.

It's not the way I would choose on my own; it's likely not the approach you would opt for either. But His ways are above ours. They don't always make sense to us, similar to how the life of Jesus doesn't make sense to anyone seeking a life of comfort and worldly success. There is truly no one like the Lord Jesus Christ.

**ROMANS 7:24-25**

O wretched man that I am! who shall deliver me from the body of this death? I thank God through Jesus Christ our Lord. So then with the mind I myself serve the law of God; but with the flesh the law of sin.

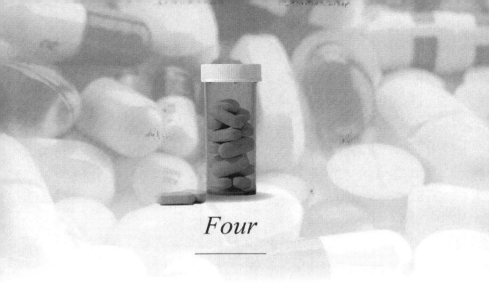

# *Four*

# ADDICTION
# A Dangerous Friend

THE MOMENT I CLOSED THE DOOR, I knew something was off. The inside of our house was usually filled with the most wonderful aromas emanating from my mother's potpourri throughout the house. Over the background sounds of the living room television, I often heard the bustle of work somewhere in the house. The running of the vacuum. The tinkle of silverware. The splash of water in the sink. My mother was constantly cleaning.

Today, I heard nothing. Silence. Complete auditory darkness.

"Hello?" I called as I walked through the back door into the kitchen.

I walked through the loud, yellow-painted kitchen and into the dining room and dropped my backpack on a nearby chair. The house was quiet. My mother always was around to greet me when I got home from school. Today, she was nowhere to be found.

I moved slowly, like a prowler in my own home, listening for the faintest sound. Still, there was nothing. Not a peep from anyone, anywhere in the place.

I swallowed, my throat dry. "Anyone home?"

A shadow moved, blocking the light from the front living room windows. Someone *was* here, walking toward the stairs in the living room.

"Mother?" I said, moving toward the archway past the dining room table. "Is everything okay?"

It was my father. He turned and walked back down the stairs toward me.

"Hey, dad," I said, "where's mother?"

My father's eyes sank at the question. His face was off-white. I could tell he was preoccupied about something and instinctively I reached out to greet him with a hug.

"Come outside," he said, moving away before I could embrace him.

"Let's go sit on the back deck."

As we walked back through the dining room and kitchen, we headed out the back door onto the deck, where I saw my brother, John, walking up the deck steps.

"John?" I beckoned. "What's going on?" John didn't respond, sullenly taking a seat.

"Just… just sit," my father stammered. He pointed hastily at a chair and then took his own seat.

I rushed to my place and took it. I didn't want to delay this news, however terrible, any longer.

"What is it?" I said. "Come on, just tell me."

Dad looked at John as if the two of them were keeping a secret from me. But then he lifted his gaze to meet mine, and I realized that the dark truth to be revealed had nothing to do with me.

"Mother's not here," he said, voice quivering. "She... she's had to go away for a while."

"Go away?" I echoed, confused. "Where?"

"To a rehabilitation center."

I blinked, and a booming voice in my head screamed, *What? Why? This doesn't make sense!*

"What?" I said. "I don't understand."

My father looked at me and shook his head.

I looked at my brother, who was looking me straight in the face. "It's true, Lawrence," he said.

At this, my father bowed his head again and sniffed.

"I don't get it," I said, my heart pounding. "Why? What for?"

"You know mother's back pain?"

"Yes."

"You know how she takes pills to deal with it?"

I nodded, my head almost flying off my neck. "Sure!" I said. "Of course she does. Some days she can hardly bear the pain."

"Yes," John continued, "but—"

"She needs them," I interrupted, my cheeks burning. "Don't you see how much pain she's in? Just the other day,

John, she couldn't hold your baby because of how bad it was. Remember how she's been slurring her speech a lot lately? Huh?"

"Lawrence," he said, trying to get my attention. But I was confused and wondered why they spoke ill of the most cherished person in my life. My mother was an angel in my eyes. She was perfect. I wanted to say something, but I just sat there eerily quiet, unlike my usual talkative self.

"Lawrence," John said.

"What?"

"Listen to us," he said. "Mother didn't have trouble holding baby Marcus because of her back pain. It was because she was on too many pills."

My dad sniffed again, his nose full of fresh mucus. He pulled a handkerchief from his pocket and blew it with a loud burst.

"That doesn't make sense," I said, looking back at my brother.

"It makes complete sense, Lawrence," my brother said. "Slurred speech? Constantly rubbing an itchy nose?" He cocked his head, as if to get me to admit he was right.

"Yeah," I said with a shrug. "So?"

"That's not from the pain," John said. "It's from taking too many painkillers."

"What do you mean, 'too many?'"

John took a breath and exhaled slowly. "She's addicted to them, Lawrence. She has been for years, and she needs help."

"Then help her," I spat. "Why send her away?"

At this, my father spoke. *"We didn't."*

I turned to him to find his eyes boring into mine, wide and red with tears. "You didn't?" I stammered.

"I would never send your mother away," he declared.

Then I realized what I had just done. I had questioned my dad's loyalty to her. I had challenged his love of his bride.

*She had volunteered to go.*

"Dad," I said, the hot rush of my tears rising fast, "I'm so sorry!"

"Your mother loves you guys very much," my dad continued. "But these pills have taken control of her life, and she desires to get better so she can come back home and be the mother she wants to be."

It was then that I embraced him. I felt his hands take me back. We hugged each other. Then my dad suggested, "Why don't the three of us have a men's meal since mother is absent." We all went back into the house, and dad did something unusual. He cooked us dinner that night.

I'll always remember that.

M Y MOTHER NEARLY DIED giving birth to me. My mother's last trimester was particularly arduous as the doctor directed her to remain in bed to avoid losing me. She spent the last two months of her pregnancy bedridden. And when complications worsened, she was hospitalized for a long four weeks and constantly monitored, not even permitted to get up to use the restroom. The physicians were concerned for her life and mine, as there was a serious possibility she would hemorrhage and bleed to death.

Sure enough, during the delivery, my mother began to bleed profusely. The doctors quickly grabbed life-saving utensils, performed an emergency C-section, and focused on reviving her weakened body. According to my father, it was pretty frightening for a few minutes. However, thankfully after yanking me out of her womb, the doctors could stop the blood loss and stabilize her.

My mother played an essential role in shaping me into the person I am. She has been my closest confidant, offering unwavering support, advice, and comfort whenever needed. Her listening ear, warm hugs, and affectionate kisses have been invaluable to me. I hold her in the highest regard and feel truly blessed God preserved her life.

When my brother and I were young, my mother made it a priority to take us to church. She believed in sowing a foundation of faith and knowledge about Jesus Christ into our lives. This was no small feat, considering she also dealt with severe back pain and other physical ailments. Over time, her scoliosis worsened, leading to intense throbbing throughout her body that required prescription opiate medications to manage. Unfortunately, this led to another problem: addiction. Over the next decade, my mother became increasingly dependent on these pills, requiring higher and higher doses to manage her miserable pain.

Until that moment on the back deck, I was unaware of my mother's addiction. I rarely remember seeing her take any pills, likely because the act was insignificant in my naive eyes. Taking medications was something all grownups did. Besides, if I did witness her abusing her pain pills, I have no memory of it. Perhaps I was blinded by her unwavering love and care for me, or maybe God erased these memories.

However, I remember accompanying her to pick up medication at dank, poorly-kept medical clinics in poorer neighborhoods of Columbus. She filled her monthly prescriptions at standard pharmacies, yet still had to travel across town to these creepy locales. She also took me to "friends' houses" to get the rest of her supposed prescription. Somehow these friends were never people who came to our home or church; I never saw them aside from these visits. Their presence gnawed at me. I got the same uncomfortable feeling around them as when that man would put his hands on me and act as if I wanted it. I could tell they were not trustworthy people.

One day, my mother's addiction put me in strange jeopardy. We walked to the house of a neighbor who was also one of my mother's "friends," she told me to play with the neighbor's two daughters. I knew the girls from school and saw them around the neighborhood, and I was quite excited: I found one of them very attractive! Sadly for me, she did not reciprocate.

With the living room TV blaring, my mother and the neighbor went into the back kitchen to talk, leaving me with their other daughter, Hollie. Hollie was a little older than me, and very fat, if I may be blunt. Since the adults were busy, she invited me upstairs to her room to hang out and watch TV. Once we were in her room, I was surprised to find another girl there, a friend of Hollie's. The friend also happened to be a big girl, and her demeanor creeped me out. She shut the door as I walked around the room, looking at Hollie's things. Out of nowhere, Hollie suddenly pushed me onto the bed and pinned me down. Despite my pleas for her to stop, she continued to smother me. I gasped for air but couldn't breathe. I tried to scream, only for the sound to disappear into her torso.

I reached out to Hollie's friend, who was sitting across the room, watching with a cruel smile on her face. I stretched my fingers toward her, hoping she'd help me.

Instead, she turned on the TV and raised the volume to its maximum. Then she laughed at me.

"We're going to have sex!" Hollie uttered in my ear, her breath hot.

"No!" I cried. "Please, no!"

I was petrified. I was a virgin and had no desire to break my virginity.

"Come on, it'll be fun!" Hollie's friend jeered.

Hollie laughed even louder, pressing herself onto me.

"No, no, please!"

I kicked and pushed as hard as I could. By some miracle, I wriggled under her to the edge of the bed and rolled out onto the floor. I scrambled to my feet, flew to the door, and ran out as fast as possible.

My feet thundering, I sprinted down the stairs as my mother walked into the messy living room.

"I'm going home!" I yelled.

"Why?" she said, gulping.

"Home!" I cried, and I flew from the house and let the door slam behind me.

MY MOTHER'S ADDICTION was a source of terrible tension between her and my father. He was a relatively new convert to Christ, yet he modeled Christ's love brilliantly. He did his best to support her and cope with her problems. Still, they argued constantly. My mother had become very good at concealing her pills, and she often yelled and fought with my father as he searched the house for them.

Looking back, I realize he was torn between supporting and enabling her. He did his best to hold her accountable, often searching the house for stowed pills. He would discover pill bottles hidden in unlikely places, like shoes, jewelry boxes, and even kitchen cups stored on the upper shelves. My mother would plead with him not to throw them away, sobbing uncontrollably.

I didn't understand why he would get so angry with her, and so much of my childhood was spent harboring frustration toward my father. My mother was in a lot of pain, and I believed taking pills was a reasonable solution. However, my father recognized she had lost control of her addiction.

When he and my brother, John, broke the news at the impressionable age of 15, I had to accept my reality wasn't what I thought it was. My mother's life was spiraling out of control. She was an addict, and while I loved her deeply, that addiction was dangerous for us all.

It was difficult to accept. My mother was a saint, an angel in my eyes. I longed for a closer relationship with my father during my childhood. I wish he had been more assertive in pursuing a relationship with me, and I wish my mother had encouraged him to do so. That way, I would have had a healthier, more balanced set of influences growing up.

That didn't change how much I loved her. She was my rock, my biggest supporter. By God's grace, she still is the most important woman in my life today.

But she needed her loved ones to tell her the truth, not shower her with endless compliments and praises. Yes, she needed encouragement, but she didn't need flattery. My mother was at war with a deadly addiction, and if we didn't all band together to support her, we might have lost her forever.

JAMES 4:6

But he giveth more grace.
Wherefore he saith, God
resisteth the proud, but giveth
grace unto the humble.

## *Have You Considered*

---

# Why Is This Happening
# to My Loved One?

IT'S NOT EASY to care for an addict. Someone you love is struggling through a period of immense suffering. The instinct to ease the pain and provide comfort is overwhelming.

Yet, for many addicts, more "comfort" is the worst thing we can offer. Someone in my mother's position, a person with a legitimate need for painkillers, didn't need comfort; she needed restraint and self-discipline.

When these situations arise, we must resist the temptation to isolate ourselves. Addiction can seem incredibly shameful, and like my admission of same-sex attraction, it can draw criticism toward us. If we genuinely want to support our loved ones in their need, we must gather courage and face the doubters—or better yet, ignore them. People who slander someone battling addiction are ignorant of the gospel.

Consider when Jesus said, "They that are whole have no need of the physician, but they that are sick: I came not to call the righteous, but sinners to repentance." (Mark 2:17). My mother was sick and needed a physician. Your loved one (or even you) may be in a death match with addiction. We need help from those who can offer it, not armchair quarterbacking from critics unwilling to lift a finger to help.

Don't lock yourself away while treating and caring for an addict; instead, call out for help and rally a team around you. In these trying times, forming a supportive network becomes paramount, as addiction thrives in loneliness. It's essential to gather friends and family as pillars of strength, offering practical assistance such as making meals, providing rides to and from work or treatment, and simply being compassionate friends to stave off loneliness, one of the most challenging triggers for someone struggling with addiction.

Best of all, this team can function as a bedrock of prayer. Prayer becomes the cornerstone, knitting the threads of hope and healing together. Like physical pain and grotesque abuse, addiction is a call to depend on the Lord. All addiction is an attempt to find peace by worldly means. Alcohol, food, drugs, painkillers, gambling, and sex: Each provides an intense and immediate dose of pleasure, followed by a long hangover of dissatisfaction, guilt, and regret. They seem like quick, easy solutions to life's problems; in reality, they complicate those problems.

To fight addiction, we need physical *and* spiritual treatment. Chemical addiction requires its own particular approach (such as a stint in rehab), but all addiction is a spiritual illness that can only be healed by the Great Physician. The only way we gain access to His care is to stop trying to get treatment elsewhere. In other words, stop going to the pharmacy when you need the emergency room!

Prayer is the most powerful means to win the spiritual war against addiction. The Holy Spirit is mighty and possesses the strength to heal sin and mend brokenness *if we depend on Him.* God wants to be everything to us, and during these moments of desperate need, we are reminded of the extent of our helplessness when standing alone. Genuine faith grows stronger as we seek God's strength to overcome worldliness and independence, placing our complete trust in Him.

In these times of immense challenge and confusion, we often find ourselves searching for a source of unwavering strength and guidance. In these moments, turning to the Holy Bible will provide an anchor of comfort and encouragement. The Scriptures hold a treasure trove of precious promises from God that speak directly to our struggles and pains.

Just as your dedication to helping your loved one is unyielding, so too can be your reliance on the wisdom and promises contained within God's Word. Through daily immersion in the Word, you open God's pages to a wellspring of hope, courage, and resilience. The stories of redemption, forgiveness, and transformative healing found within the Bible remind us that, even in the face of insurmountable challenges, God's strength stands ready to uplift and sustain us. Each moment we spend in the Bible feeds our spirit with truth, strength, and power. This helps us face each day with stronger faith and steadfast determination as we continue to support and uplift our loved ones in their journey to recovery.

I am so grateful for my mother's courage and commitment to receive treatment. Because of her humility and honesty, she learned how to control her medication use. This means she experiences much more body pain than she'd prefer. Countless times she has shed tears and called out to the Lord for strength. I have watched her lay in bed in agonizing pain, which has strengthened her faith over the years. In turn, this has encouraged me to endure my own mental and spiritual struggles. Thus a chain of exhortation and hope has formed between us as we labor together for the good of the gospel and the purity of our faith.

Love has a way of making our pains more bearable. When we anchor our trust in the Lord, remembering His beloved Son's life, death, and resurrection, we gain the fortitude to endure suffering with joy and courage. For His sake, we can console ourselves and each other, even in the darkest hours of lonely suffering.

Don't let addiction be the conqueror. You are not alone. Your loved one is not alone.

Jesus is with you, and He loved sinners so much that He lived alongside them, taught them, healed them, and paid the ultimate price for their destructive sins.

In moments of desperation, call out to the One who is able. Cry out to Christ, over and over. Let your cries sound before God's throne, embracing Christ's strength and promises, depending on Him entirely. Only then can the suffering of addiction become a beautiful story of triumph.

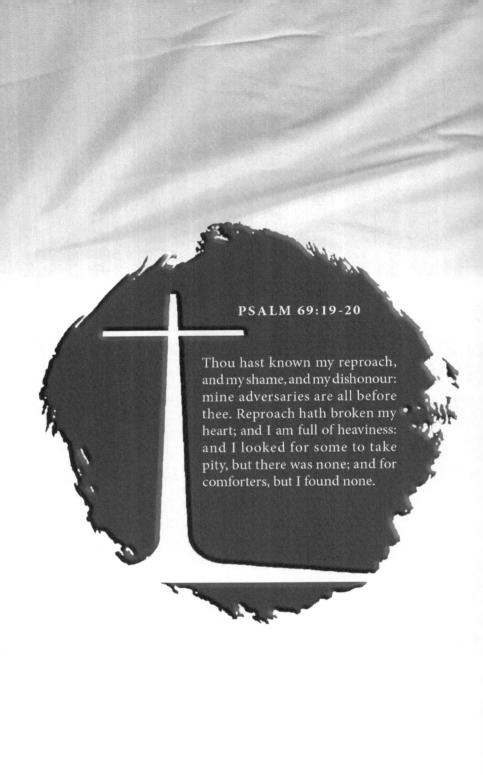

**PSALM 69:19-20**

Thou hast known my reproach, and my shame, and my dishonour: mine adversaries are all before thee. Reproach hath broken my heart; and I am full of heaviness: and I looked for some to take pity, but there was none; and for comforters, but I found none.

## *Five*

---

# S H A M E
# Run and Hide

TOMATO SOUP is so much worse on the way up! But that's what David's mom was serving, so I ate it.

As a good Midwestern boy, I was raised to be polite and gracious when visiting a friend's house. One didn't question or refuse the entrée being offered. I choked down the thick, acidic brew with the strongest smile I could muster, yet mere minutes after the stuff hit my stomach, I felt the rumbling begin.

*Just make it to bedtime,* I told myself.

We played a few more games with David's older siblings, John and Dawn. My stomach seemed to settle down as the night wore on.

"Why don't you sleep in John's bed?" their mother offered.

"That's okay," I said.

"Go ahead," John said. "I'll just put a movie on and crash on the couch."

"No movies, young man!" his mother chided him, but he just laughed and headed off, leaving his bed to me.

It was a nice-sized bed, super comfortable with soft sheets. I loved it, and I was asleep within minutes of turning out the lights.

But the tomato soup wasn't going down so easily.

I slept for a few hours before waking up to the sensation of barbed wire looping through my stomach.

*I'm going to throw up.*

I threw John's bedsheets off and scrambled down the hall, groping in the dark along the walls to find the bathroom.

*Hurry, Lawrence, hurry—*

The first wave erupted out of my system, hot and sour like an acidic volcano. I tried to cover my mouth, but vomit spewed between my fingers all over my friends' hallway floor and further into the bathroom.

Immediately lights began to click on.

*No, no!*

I scurried up off the floor and grabbed a towel from the rack.

"Lawrence?" a voice called. "Is that you?"

It was David.

"Yeah, no..." I said. "I'm... I'm fine—"

*Blech!*

Another surge of stomach fluid rushed out of me and

spattered on the bathroom tile, missing the commode. It was so gross! The filthy scarlet and gold miasma was all over the floor, with little splotches on the cupboards and walls. My shirt was a mess with it, too, and my pajama bottoms—

I gaped at my thin trousers. They, too, were soaking wet. But not with tomato puke.

"Oh, man!" I heard a voice say back in John's room. "It's all over the bed!"

"God, no..." I whispered.

*Run.*

I looked out into the hall and then back into the bathroom. Maybe I could shower it off? I had to do something to cover this up, to hide the fact that I had just—

"Lawrence?" David called. "Are you okay?"

*Hide.*

"I'm... I'm good!" I shouted, turning on the hot water. "I got sick. I need a shower, okay?"

My friend appeared at the door, took one look at the mess of vomit, and winced. "Yikes... you vomited all over the hallway, too."

"Sorry," I moaned. I climbed into the bathtub in full clothing, hoping to rinse it off somehow.

"Hey buddy," David said, raising his voice above the sound of the spraying water. "Did you puke in John's bed?"

"I... um... maybe," I stammered.

*My pants were soaked. It was like I had unleashed Niagara in the middle of the night—*

"It doesn't look like puke," David said. "Or smell like it."

I froze, the water streaming over my face. I didn't answer.

"Lawrence?"

"Yeah?"

"What's in John's bed?"

I swallowed.

*Don't tell the truth, don't tell the truth, don't you DARE tell the truth—*

"I... I don't know."

"It smells like pee, man."

I wanted to drop dead.

"No, it doesn't," I lied.

"Um, yeah, it does," David answered.

Then he said nothing more, walking back to his brother's room to clean the sheets I had soiled with buckets of urine.

I stood with my pajamas on in that shower for a seeming eternity. I never wanted to leave it. I never wanted to face David, John, or his family again.

But I would have to. And when I did, my years-long secret would be out in the open, never to be hidden again.

IT ALL STARTED with my abuse. My parents didn't know it, but the timing was unmistakable. My body, and the part of God's Spirit that lived inside me, was crying out against the evils done to me by my abuser. Mother and dad assumed it was because I was a heavy sleeper and couldn't make it to the bathroom in time. From age four all the way until college, I was a serial bedwetter, prohibiting me from enjoying many of the pleasures of boyhood.

I longed to go on outings like camping trips with my schoolmates or stay over at a friends' homes. Despite my yearning to join in many overnight adventures, my parents were too afraid that I would have an accident in the middle of the night. They opted to keep me home. It was simply too risky.

The one time they loosened this protective net—the only time, in fact—was the time I begged to go to David's house. It ended horribly and crushed any chances of participating in overnight activities for the foreseeable future.

I was particularly heartbroken when my school conducted a raffle, the winner of which received a free week-long camping excursion with the school. It was over in the mountains of West Virginia, a place I have always been fond of, and it wasn't cheap. Mother and dad always opted out of the annual affair, claiming it was too expensive. But this year, the school held a raffle, and my name was drawn. I was ecstatic and hurried home to tell my parents the news.

Holding the winning certificate in her hands, my mother sat down and placed her fingers over her mouth, perhaps stifling a small burst of emotion.

"We can't go, baby," she muttered.

"What?" I cried. "Of course, we can. I won!"

My mother turned to me and shook her head.

"Lawrence. It's a week of camping."

"Yeah?" I said.

"A week with your classmates. *Many* of them."

It began to sink in. I'd never make it a week without peeing the bed. Getting through a single night was still considered a monumental achievement in my household. What were we supposed to do? Bring seven sleeping bags just for me?

I burst into tears, yelled something about it not being fair, ran to my room, and slammed the door. I wanted to stay mad at my mother, to make it her fault, but I knew the truth. I couldn't go. The bullying would be relentless. I'd be an outcast. No longer would a limited group of people like David and his family know; *everyone* would know. I had to keep trying to hide my secret.

I hadn't yet made the connection between the bedwetting and the abuse I suffered as a young child. From my point of view, the bedwetting was my fault.

Something was wrong *with me.*

So it was that throughout my adolescence, I was constantly yoked with terrible shame.

It's challenging to speak about how difficult this was for me. There were so many nights I would lie in my bed crying, unwilling to fall asleep for fear of the embarrassment that was to come.

Many of those nights, I was alone. My brother always got to spend nights with his friends without any worries or objections from mother and dad. He attended overnight trips to amusement parks and participated in school and church trips. I never got to enjoy these experiences, all because of the relentless brokenness my body had suffered.

I can't fully express the pain I would feel. I used to pray to God and ask, "Why am I wetting the bed?" Every morning I'd be so embarrassed because my mother had to wash the sheets *and* the waterproof pads she'd cover the bed with. Especially as I grew into a teenager, the mess wasn't just a spot or section of my pajamas. It was *everywhere*.

If I was embarrassed to face my poor mother each morning, it pained me to see the look on my dad's face each morning. I don't know if he intended it, but I perceived nothing but pure disappointment from him.

My parents didn't merely attempt to hide the problem. We visited a lot of doctors' offices, hoping to get answers. The medical professionals had me try various alarm clocks and smart pads, and prescribed medications. When those approaches proved ineffective, they advised my parents to restrict my water intake after 8:00. When that wasn't early enough, the doctors pushed it back to 7:00, then 6:00. Like any active kid, I got thirsty, but my parents refused. I'd have to sneak just to get a sip of water.

The one time we did an overnight and I *didn't* pee was on a camping trip with some friends. We stayed in an RV, and my mother took it upon herself to ensure I didn't pee that night. I didn't have a drop of water after 6:00, and my mother kept me up until 11:00 to make sure my bladder was empty. I went to bed, praying that night would be different.

Yet I woke, hardly an hour or two later, to her stroking my cheek.

"Sweetheart," she whispered, "it's time to get up."

I blinked and looked around. The RV was still pitch black.

"Is… is it morning?" I mumbled.

"No, no," she said. "It's time to get up and go to the bathroom."

I sighed, the heaviness of my awful problem landing on me again. Without a word, I rose, shuffled to the tiny RV bathroom, and forced out whatever liquid was left inside me. Mother marched me back to bed, kissed me on the forehead, and promised to wake me again in an hour or so.

I didn't pee that night only because of my mother. I didn't sleep much either, but neither did she.

Such was the price a single night of dry sheets cost her.

IMAGINE THE LONELINESS I FELT. Imagine the embarrassment, the constant humiliation, the ongoing sense that something in me was broken, unlike with anyone else. The continuous voice tells you to run and hide, to protect yourself from drowning.

Perhaps you have endured suffering like this. Maybe you've experienced ridicule and scorn. We all go through middle school, so it's safe to assume you were picked on for something. Adolescence can be a challenge of teasing and mockery. Bullies will find any reason to target and hurl insults at you. When we are teased, it's easy to feel deep shame based on what they say.

Unfortunately, at the age when teasing is most prevalent, we know little of psychology. Few eleven and twelve-year-olds have the wherewithal to call a bully out for what they truly are—a coward. Almost no young person realizes bullies are acting out of their own insecurities and shame, and will do practically anything to move those negative feelings elsewhere.

I wasn't teased about bedwetting too often. Miraculously, few people knew about it. One person, however, knew about it.

My dear, wonderful grandfather.

As bedwetting persisted into high school, it became my custom to wear adult diapers each night to prevent soiling the bed sheets. It was a humiliating experience, as each morning I had to dispose of the wet diaper in the bathroom trash can before taking a shower. It was a constant reminder of my inability to control something most people take for granted.

My grandparents were up visiting us for a week in Columbus and staying in our house. My grandfather possessed a most gentle and kind temperament and was someone I looked up to and admired. He was almost always a soft-spoken and gracious man, but one morning, he couldn't contain his annoyance any longer when he saw me dispose of the wet diaper. He came over, retrieved the thick wad from the waste bin, and thrust it into my face.

"What's wrong with you?" he growled. "Why don't you just get up and pee in the toilet like a normal boy?"

I didn't know what to say. This was so out of character for him. Hot shock paralyzed me from feet to forehead, so I just stared blankly at him.

Apparently, my silence did nothing to soften his aggravation, and he hurled the diaper back into the trash and walked away.

As he departed, overwhelming shame fell on me like a lead coat. I wanted to curl up on the ground and sob.

What was wrong with me? Why was I broken? Why couldn't I control this issue, this gross and childish and embarrassing habit?

And why would God let it go on for so long? Didn't He love me and want me to live a normal life?

THANKFULLY THE BEDWETTING STOPPED. At the perfect time, too, I might add.

When I moved into my college dormitory as a freshman, my body quickly stopped peeing at night. I don't know why, but I have a guess: I was no longer near the reminders of my abuser.

I was a man, a free adult with agency over my life. Something inside me no longer needed to cope with the trauma, and I could finally enjoy a vibrant social life.

Several years later, while still in my college studies, I discovered the underlying cause of my bedwetting as I realized what my abuser had done to me. This was a startling yet liberating experience for me. Previously I had held myself responsible for my bedwetting, believing it to be a personal failure. Now I understood it was a symptom of a much larger issue that was not my fault. Despite the difficulties and frustrations I experienced, I am grateful for the clarity and insight it gave me. I believe that my exclusion from many childhood activities was a way for God to draw me closer to Him. Perhaps this is why, as a child, I yearned to know God as a friend more than most teenagers do.

On a final note, I want to make sure the following is clear: Persistent bedwetting is a sign of sexual abuse. It's one of the easiest signs to see and should cause parents and guardians to take a closer look at who is around their children.

With that in mind, I do wish my parents had recognized the warning signs of sexual abuse and sought help earlier on. However, I don't fault them one bit. Predators are exceptionally skilled at manipulating trust for their evil exploits.

I am thankful for the unwavering patience and support both my parents gave me, even though they could not fully comprehend the underlying problem. It's always tempting to assign blame, but as I wrote before, assigning blame is the easy part. It never brings healing. It may bring clarity, but never closure.

Thankfully, I've been walking with the Lord to heal from the trauma of my abuse and the numerous embarrassing situations that abuse spawned. I hope you come to Jesus with whatever trauma you've endured. I hope you will resist Satan's accusations and trust Jesus enough not to run, hide, and avoid the healing process.

You can rest on the courage of Jesus Christ. No man has ever endured so much with such strength. No one has ever transformed worldly shame into eternal glory so beautifully.

Jesus offers us that power if we trust Him and depend on Him fully.

You can trust Him.

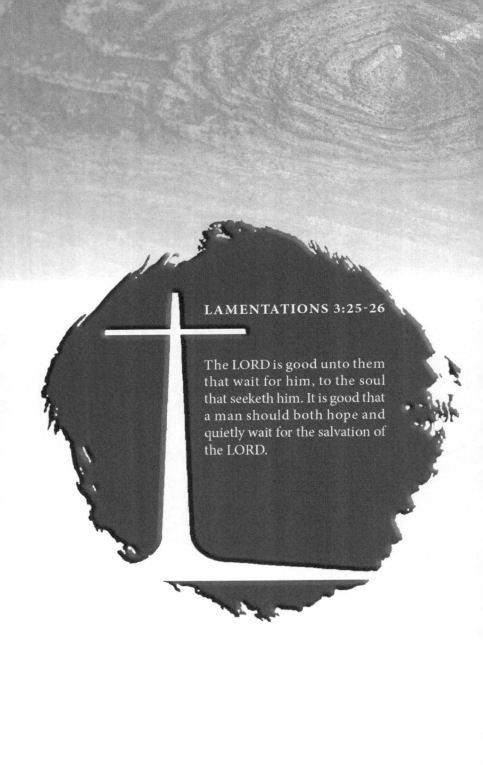

**LAMENTATIONS 3:25-26**

The LORD is good unto them
that wait for him, to the soul
that seeketh him. It is good that
a man should both hope and
quietly wait for the salvation of
the LORD.

# Where Is God
# When I'm Suffering?

IT'S EASY to think God has abandoned us. When we are at our lowest, and the pain is most intense, one can easily feel God has forsaken us.

Yet Scripture is clear our God does not abandon us during times of immense suffering; rather, this is when He is *closest* to us.

The writer of Hebrews declares, "For in that he himself [Jesus] hath suffered being tempted, he is able to succour them that are tempted" (Hebrews 2:18). Succour means running to and compassionately supporting, aiding, and providing help in times of distress.

As a man, Jesus experienced the points of temptations we experience in suffering. He was touched by the feelings of our infirmities. He was subjected to shameful situations and endured them only as God could.

While I doubt Jesus struggled with bedwetting as I did, He was subjected to plenty of shame given the context He lived in. As Jesus approached age 30, He would have already gained recognition as a good teacher in Israel under Roman occupation rule. According to the prevailing religious culture, reaching this milestone meant assuming a more prominent role in ministry. He was expected to build a following of educated, well-connected religious leaders. Instead, he chose fishermen, a tax collector, and some of the "deplorables" of that day. He wasn't concerned with public reputation whatsoever, leading to many moments where he was the target of much indignation.

During His triumphal entry into Jerusalem, Jesus opted to ride on the back of a donkey. In those days, kings and leaders always aimed to project strength. The preferable beast of burden was a horse, preferably an enormous one at that.

But a donkey? An *ass*? Jesus chose to fulfill Scripture rather than public expectations and enter the capital city as a servant, not a slayer. As the prophet Zechariah wrote, "Rejoice greatly, O daughter of Zion; shout, O daughter of Jerusalem: behold, thy King cometh unto thee: he is just, and having salvation; lowly, and riding upon an ass, and upon a colt the foal of an ass" (Zechariah 9:9). Jesus humbly rode into Jerusalem in a manner that deliberately shunned the power structure of the day, signaling His intention to lead through sacrifice, rather than conquest.

Waiting for Jesus in the city of Jerusalem was His

greatest "shame": The Cross.

While the Christian cross has become a familiar symbol over the last two thousand years, in Jesus' day, it was not a sign of faith, hope, or religion. Rather, it was the looming image of Rome's dreadful power. It hung over Israel like the Grim Reaper's scythe. When criminals were hanged upon it, the only outcome was death. They were stripped naked and beaten within inches of their lives. Torture at its finest! Written descriptions of their crimes were nailed to the cross above them, warning passersby of the penalties for such behavior. Crosses were placed at well-trafficked crossroads and gateways, maximizing their impact. Then, as they hung there, the victims either suffocated or bled to death in a most cruel and agonizing fashion, all while the world looked on. In Jesus' day, there was no worse shameful death than death on the Roman cross.

One must also remember the timeless idea of glory, uniquely reserved for death in battle. Consider great Greek epics in which heroes boast of their deeds and their hope to die *gloriously*, meaning in combat. To die a hero's death in battle, even by one's own sword, is to win eternal glory. But to be captured, tortured, and executed by the opposing king is an utter shame.

With that in mind, think about what Jesus did. His people expected Him to enter Jerusalem as a warrior, to defeat the Romans and overthrow the governor, Pontius Pilate. Yet Jesus entered humbly, as a lowly servant, and allowed a close friend to betray Him. When falsely accused of crimes, Jesus said nothing in His defense. He submitted Himself to the judgment of Pontius Pilate, the ruler of the enemy, who crucified Him.

A notable plot twist occurs in this part of the story. In those days, it was customary to release one prisoner during the Jewish feast of Passover. At the time, Pilate had two: Jesus and Barabbas, an insurrectionist. The people chose Barabbas, a man with a plot that led him to murder and attempt to overthrow Roman rule.

Having released his customary prisoner, Pilate ordered that Jesus be disrobed, savagely flogged, and paraded to Golgotha to be nailed to the tree beside two malicious criminals.

In a worldly sense, can you imagine greater shame? Can you picture a defeat more disgraceful?

Yet when we shift our perspective to that of Heaven, considering Jesus' astounding mission to save sinners, can you think of anyone braver than He? Can you imagine the courage this required?

Jesus had no concern for worldly glory and worldly shame. Rather, He embraced worldly shame because He knew it would lead to eternal glory.

So how do we empathize with those who suffer? How do we acquaint ourselves with shame when every bone in our body cries out against it?

We must look at the Suffering Saviour, the Man of Sorrows, and the Lamb of God as our example. We must behold His shame and marvel at His magnificent glory. We must believe our shame is temporary and fleeting as long as we seek His glory that remains steady, unaffected by the validation of bullies and gossip. Our place is by the foot of the cross, where we must stay.

Bedwetting was a extreme challenge for me. It was humiliating, constantly hampering my childhood. I spent many nights secretly crying due to utter shame. It deprived me of many positive experiences I longed to share with my brother and friends.

However, God has used these traumatic memories, feelings of loneliness, shame, and guilt to cultivate in me an invaluable treasure of compassion, patience, and understanding toward others. I am truly grateful to God for isolating me so He could develop these precious treasures. Today, I am in a healthier emotional and mental state, and I have faith He will continue to work in my life for good.

So how can we feel God's presence during immense suffering? What can we do to feel His loving kindness and healing touch?

We must look to Christ and His Holy Bible. Within His Word, we find encouragement from the testimonies of our suffering *brethren*, those who came before us and endured unspeakable alienation and hurt.

One of the greatest biblical characters to inspire sufferers is King David, the "man after God's own heart," who was Israel's leader for several tumultuous years.

In Psalm 13, David expressed his heart and wrote: *"How long wilt thou forget me, O LORD?* for ever? how long wilt thou hide thy face from me? How long shall I take counsel in my soul, having sorrow in my heart daily? how long shall mine enemy be exalted over me? Consider and hear me, O LORD my God: lighten mine eyes, lest I sleep the sleep of death; Lest mine enemy say, I have prevailed against him; and those that trouble me rejoice when I am moved. But I have trusted in thy mercy; my heart shall rejoice in thy salvation. *I will sing unto the LORD, because he hath dealt bountifully with me"* (emphasis added).

As David wrote these words, he was running for his life. The current king, Saul, had gone mad with jealousy. David was the next chosen king, but Saul, like any power-hungry authoritarian, was not interested in yielding the throne to this upstart boy from the countryside. Saul's fury was so extreme that David became a black spot in society; people in the kingdom were afraid to associate with David, fearing they would become the target of the king's irrational judgment.

David fled from Jerusalem and found shelter in a cave outside a town called Adullam. While four hundred loyal but disheartened soldiers supported him, his heart was lonely and defeated. Hadn't God just promised to make him the chosen king of Israel? It was mere months earlier that he had defeated the foul-mouthed giant Goliath in battle, winning glory and praise from everyone in the kingdom. Why was this happening to him?

David certainly felt his life was over and God had abandoned him and taken his misery to the page when he penned Psalm 13. Thankfully, our God is patient and understanding. He grasps that we sometimes feel alone and perplexed. We too may be stuck in our own caves, crying out for mercy.

Perhaps you can empathize with David. You're in a place where your emotions, circumstances, and well-being are disconnected from others and God. Like David, you look at your life and wonder, "What is happening?" "Why am I forgotten?" "Where is God?" You might even feel like you can't go on.

God knows these times will come. Part of the reason He knows is because He suffered too.

Prior to Jesus' arrest and crucifixion, He went to the Garden of Gethsemane to pray. Jesus expressed to his disciples, "My soul is exceeding sorrowful, even unto death." And then he went a little further, and fell on his face, and prayed, saying, "O my Father, if it be possible, let this cup pass from me: nevertheless not as I will, but as thou wilt" (Matthew 26:38-39).

Yet a few hours later, Jesus would hear nothing but silence from His Heavenly Father. While hanging on the cross, suffering unspeakable agony for sins He did not commit, Jesus cried, "Eli, Eli, lama sabachthani?" that is to say, "My God, my God, why hast thou forsaken me?" (Matthew 27:46).

*Forsaken.*

Jesus was abandoned by His Father. Discarded. Rejected. All to pay for the sins of the very people who had nailed Him to that bloody tree.

Jesus can empathize with your suffering because He has been there.

He also offers us amazing hope. A mere three days later, Jesus rose from the dead and walked out of the tomb, risen to life by the Father's power and the Spirit's presence. Jesus conquered death so you and I may enter God's eternal rest!

There will undoubtedly be times when we feel like David and cry aloud, "How long wilt thou forget me, O Lord?" We feel abandoned and forgotten and wonder if it's because we're just too sinful or shameful for His love anymore.

Yet Jesus took all our guilt and shame upon Himself on the cross. There is no longer any reason you cannot look the Father in the face, and He calls you *Beloved*.

You may be experiencing a season where you sense God's voice in ways that seem unfamiliar. His presence and provision may show itself in unexpected manners. I can't count the times I thought God had abandoned me, only to look back later and see all the ways He had been there all along, showering me with love and comfort in ways I couldn't imagine.

When you and I find ourselves in an emotional meltdown—feeling disillusioned as if all the world has turned upside down and God has abandoned us—we quickly need to stop in our tracks, take a deep breath, and come to God in prayer. I'm not talking about a quick prayer. I mean a good, long prayer—calling out to God, crying to Him, and giving all our burdens until the tears have dried up and we are immersed in His peace.

Thankfully, David's psalm provides an excellent template for such a prayer. In verse 3, he wrote, "Consider and hear me, O LORD my God: lighten mine eyes, lest I sleep the sleep of death." In his simple prayer, David asked the LORD for three things:

1. Look at me.

David felt as though God had turned His back on him, so he asked the Lord to turn around and look at him. He requested God to consider and turn His attention towards him. While we know God indeed does not turn His back on us, there are moments when it can feel that way, especially in tough times when we might feel alone. By requesting God's attention, we affirm our deep need for Him, expressing a sincere desire to be close to Him and His refuge.

Occasionally, the burdens we face can give rise to uncertainty within us, causing us to doubt and wonder if God knows about our struggles. If when we sincerely seek God to turn His face toward us and regard our helpless state, we expose our weaknesses, acknowledging our dependence on Him. This act of humility reaffirms our dependency on God and His Word to guide us through the uncertainties which lie ahead. It signifies our trust in His sovereignty and a plea for His merciful intervention. We are in need of Him. We need Him to be our strength and refuge, for the Lord is our portion; therefore, we can place our hope in Him (Lamentations 3:24).

2. Answer me.

David also felt God had ceased speaking to him, encountering a profound sense of silence. At times, God's voice may assume a whispering tone, prompting us to seek Him more earnestly and listen with heightened attentiveness. This process nurtures our ability to listen and pay closer attention to Him. Similarly, David's longing to hear God's voice once more led him to request that intimate connection, reminiscent of the relationship he had in years gone by.

Applying that today, this is a reason we should embrace a daily practice of opening the Bible. In times when we find ourselves spiritually parched, for dry seasons are inevitable, it becomes crucial to listen for His voice and fervently pray, "Grant me the light of Your Word anew. May I hold fast to Your truths. Strengthen my faith and help my unbelief!" If God is silent, there's no need for discouragement. Often, God invites us to be still and bask in silence before His presence. God is Sovereign and truly is worthy of us quieting the noise within us, sitting silently in contemplation, reverence, and patience—all in sincere dedication to listen closely... and to listen more... and sometimes to extend that listening a tad further until His Word resonates. And when God speaks, His words are profitable for reproof, correction, and wise instruction.

3. Restore me.

David's heart weighed heavy as he sensed a distant presence of God. With heartfelt pleas, he implored for the restoration of his fellowship with God. He longed for God to draw close and that God's presence would once again be near, bringing comfort and reassurance.

Let this be our prayer as well—during moments of despair or shame, may we humbly bow before God, earnestly seeking restoration. Just as David yearned for renewed closeness, let us also seek God's comforting presence to uplift and reassure us. In times of hardship and doubt, may we find the courage to pour out our pleas, confess and forsake sin, and seek fellowship with God. Then let us invite God to draw near and increase our awareness of His Spirit. As we lift our prayers, may we leave sin, doubt, and guilt behind us, at the feet of Calvary. May we believe that God's restoration will come, and our spirits will be filled with God's peace to our troubled hearts.

Believing what we pray is essential. David concluded his psalm with a note of hope: "I will sing unto the LORD, because he hath dealt bountifully with me." Though his dire situation was out of his control, David chose to believe God was at work and he still had God's favor. Despite his circumstances, he decided to praise and sing unto the Lord.

So it must be for you and me. We, too, must adopt the same attitude: To choose to believe God and trust in His love, especially when times are most challenging. Even when we don't feel like it, we must break through our reservations, open a hymnal and burst forth singing songs and praises to God. It nourishes our souls and brings honor and glory to God.

The Lord immensely loves you. He will not abandon you. Trust Him, depend on Him, and call out to Him repeatedly until you hear His gentle voice of love.

Trust me. It's always worth the wait to be brought into the arms of a loving God!

**PSALM 42:11**

Why art thou cast down, O my soul? and why art thou disquieted within me? hope thou in God: for I shall yet praise him, who is the health of my countenance, and my God.

## *Six*

---

# L O N E L I N E S S
# Drowning in Depression

WHEN I KNOCKED, MY FRIEND was quick to open the church office doors near the back of the building and let me enter.

"Good afternoon, Lawrence," he said with a smile.

"Morning," I said, the single word heavier than lead on my tongue.

I shuffled past him with a hanging head, my mind and body weary beyond comprehension.

"Have a seat, brother," he said.

I wandered through my own personal fog until I found a sofa and collapsed on its cushions. My host, a pastor who was a close confidant and friend, took a seat across from me and sat quietly in silence.

After a few minutes, he broke the silence and said,

"Brother Lawrence, what's going on?"

I lifted my head, the muscles nearly dead in my neck. I found his eyes and knew my physical gaze met his. But something in me felt like I wasn't even in the room. Like this was all a movie or dream that I'd wake up from.

I swallowed.

"I don't think you'll understand," I said, each word taxing my remaining strength. "Although I am physically here, I'm not here with you now. Not *really* here. I mean, I feel like nothing. Complete *nothingness*."

My friend listened, his face without judgment. Perhaps he thought I was crazy. If so, I was too exhausted to care.

"I... I can't even explain it," I said, my lips dry. "I'm empty... I'm *nothingness*."

My friend nodded. "I hear you," he said. Then he leaned forward, showing remarkable compassion. "I hear you, and I understand."

"You do?" I said.

He smiled. "Yes. And I'm here for you, Lawrence."

Before I knew it, I was expressing my distress, and my friend was listening attentively.

"Lawrence, there are times God allows us, and I say "us" because I'm speaking about me too, to go through seasons of nothingness. I've lived the feeling of *nothingness*. God is doing something in the midst of nothing. And it is a good thing."

His words gave me a glimpse of hope for a moment

in the deep emptiness of nothing.

After an additional quiet ten minutes together, we knelt in prayer. The only words I could muster were, "God… help." I was despondent and couldn't think of anything more to say. I didn't know how to escape the depression or even ask God. Then my friend softly prayed the exact words I needed before God's ear. The only way I was going to find true fulfillment and meaning in my desolation, would be in Christ.

After all, no one knew nothingness quite like He did.

SINCE CHILDHOOD, I'VE ALWAYS been sociable and talkative, eager to engage with others. While I wasn't timid, I sometimes felt like an outsider among my peers, wondering why some didn't want to befriend me. I was often one of the last kids chosen to play games. At the time, I wasn't aware of loneliness as a concept, so I assumed it was because I wasn't talented at sports or I was ugly. These are typical concerns many children face at school. For me, in particular, my bedwetting problem further isolated me and limited my ability to socialize with others.

However, outside of school and overnight hours, I felt at ease in my neighborhood. I regularly socialized with my peers, and enjoyed playing with friends on the streets. It wasn't until my college years that I began to have thoughts about loneliness. While I was focused on my studies and participating in various organizations on campus, I couldn't shake the feeling that I didn't quite fit in with any particular clique or group. Even as a member of various circles, I still felt like an outsider. This was my own flawed perception and manifestation of insecurity, for my peers were certainly kind and included me in activities and conversations.

It has been a number of years since my college days. Despite my active participation in various social activities and my passion for ministry work, I still struggle with a sense of not being entirely accepted and connected with others. While I try to remind myself these thoughts are unfounded and irrational, I still can't shake off the feeling of loneliness. Logically, it's unreasonable everyone on the planet dislikes me, especially considering the kindness and acceptance I have received from so many individuals in my life. Not everybody can permit me to be part of their lives yet simultaneously harbor private negative thoughts about me. However, even though I can recognize the lies and truths, I still struggle to overcome these feelings of isolation.

This insecurity or paranoia is common, especially among empathetic personalities. I care deeply about how I affect others and spend too much mental energy considering how my presence and actions impact others. Unfortunately, I tend to obsess over this relationship and react with criticism, either of myself or others. Over the years, I have gotten better. I have learned that instead of lashing out (and "lashing in" at myself), I must lean into the perfect example of Christ, who knew loneliness like no other, and who took on complete isolation for my sake on the cross.

Indeed, Jesus experienced profound loneliness throughout His life. He truly understands what the depths of being alone can feel like. Throughout His earthly journey, Jesus often faced rejection and misunderstanding from those around Him, including His family, friends, and the religious authorities. He often withdrew to pray and seek solace in His Father, as His closest disciples sometimes failed to grasp His mission.

One of the most poignant moments of Christ's loneliness occurred during His temptations in the wilderness, where Jesus was utterly alone for forty days and forty nights. To further strip away earthly comfort, the Lord fasted during this time. His only source of hope was in His Father, from whom He was apart while dwelling in human flesh.

After this long and agonizing stretch of time, Jesus finally came face to face with someone. But it wasn't a friend. It was Satan, the father of lies and the enemy of God. What followed was a near-superhuman feat of selflessness and discipline as Jesus resisted the temptations to use His divine power for selfish means, refusing food, power, and immortality one by one.

How crushing must that loneliness have felt for Him! First, to be alone and driven mad by hunger and thirst; second, to be left alone with His sworn enemy, tempting Him with remedies for hunger, thirst, and fear that would ultimately lead to a betrayal of His Heavenly Father.

Thankfully the story ends happily for Jesus and the rest of us. He refused Satan's offers and stood firm in His trust in God's Word. Satan departed, and angels immediately appeared to tend to Christ and comfort Him. He endured the trial, trusting relief was coming, and sure enough it did! What hope this offers us in our lonely suffering!

Yet this loneliness doesn't compare to the agony of Jesus' final hours. As He prayed in the Garden of Gethsemane, He found His disciples asleep, unable to fully comprehend the anguish He was experiencing. Judas' betrayal and the other disciples' desertion further deepened His sense of aloneness. Isaiah 63:3 tells us of Jesus: "I have trodden the winepress alone; and of the people there was none with me: for I will tread them in mine anger, and trample them in my fury; and their blood shall be sprinkled upon my garments, and I will stain all my raiment."

Judas infamously betrayed Jesus with a kiss. As the band of men and officers encircled Jesus to apprehend Him, His disciples abandoned Him, leaving Him to face the daunting task of redemption alone, as prophesied in the book of Isaiah. Not even those whom He had healed, raised from the dead, the blind who regained their sight, the deaf who could hear, the mute who could speak, or the poor who heard His gospel were present. His own family was also absent that fateful night, leaving Him utterly alone.

Isaiah 63:3 poignantly describes how He endured the winepress of God's wrath alone. Throughout that night and the following day, not even angels came to minister to Christ, requiring Him to march toward death in extreme isolation. During His ultimate sacrifice on the cross, no one in all creation came to His assistance, and He faced this incredible sacrifice for us *alone*.

In experiencing such profound loneliness and isolation, Jesus empathizes with all who feel abandoned and rejected. His sacrifice not only brings salvation but also serves as a reminder that He understands the depths of human suffering and loneliness, offering hope and comfort to those who may feel alone in their own struggles.

WHEN I MET WITH MY PASTOR FRIEND, the only word that came to mind about my feelings was "nothingness." I was empty because I had lost much of my social security blanket. I had friends, but I saw them sporadically and rarely connected with them meaningfully.

Throughout this season, I struggled with the crushing sensation of being so isolated on my own. It may seem obvious, but loneliness results from feeling like one is on one's own. Yet we are often surrounded by peers, friends, and family with whom we have potential for relationships. Somehow there is a disconnect between our feelings and our experiences.

I am far from the only person to feel this way. According to a lengthy report by the U.S. Surgeon General in 2023, an astounding number of Americans experience loneliness. The Surgeon General reported loneliness is plaguing half of adults and an even more significant number of young adults feel lonely.

While numerous factors contribute to this epidemic, one undeniable culprit stands out—the constant distraction of technology consumes our lives, driving us further disconnected from one another. For example, our reliance on smartphones, even for mundane tasks, has stripped away the essential elements that give human connections their significance and fulfillment. So many people consistently hold and fidget with their cell phones, even when nothing is of importance. We've lost the ability to have deep conversations, make eye contact without feeling uncomfortable, and be at peace with another person in silence. This discomfort with human interaction is taking a toll on our inner spirits, leading to isolation and loneliness, and hindering our ability to form close friendships.

I understand this is a challenge for all of us. Loneliness can feel like walking on hot coals; we'd do almost anything to get off as soon as possible!

Yet I have found deep solace in my relationship with God to persevere through loneliness. His presence becomes even more real to me as I cry out for companionship and comfort.

I have had the privilege of meeting and speaking with some exceptional men over the years who serve others in significant capacities, and many of them have expressed a sense of loneliness that comes with their work. As they take on higher levels of responsibility, the feeling of loneliness intensifies.

This seems to be one of the crosses we all must bear,

trusting in Jesus as we follow Him. This is one of the reasons I have a love-hate relationship with writing. There have been times when I have prayed to God, asking not to be burdened with the responsibility of writing another book. Accepting this task means spending countless hours alone in a room before a computer screen. Yet God doesn't agree with my prayers and once again invites me to sit down with Him and ponder, reflect, research, and write another book.

Will this suffering of loneliness ever end? I don't know in this world.

But I am confident it will end once I cross to the other side to be with Jesus and all my saved loved ones for eternity. This provides the greatest hope yet: We have a companion in Jesus right now and will have Him by our side forever! Alongside Him in Heaven, our loved ones who knew Christ as Lord will be there, too.

By communing with Jesus regularly, I find two sources of social stimulation: First, I can connect with my Creator, who loves me, and second, I am driven to share His love with others and consistently invest my life in them. We can spend precious time with Jesus by reading and meditating on His holy scriptures, specifically the stories of His life in the four Gospels. We can sing songs to Him, pray to Him, journal, go for walks, or meditate on His goodness toward us. There is almost no limit to how you can surrender your loneliness to Jesus Christ.

It's essential that we reach out to those around us and invest our lives in meaningful connections with people.

Actively cultivating genuine, close friendships with whom we can regularly socialize and create lasting memories is important. Engaging in shared activities, coming together in prayer groups, and participating in home Bible studies are all valuable ways to foster these connections. Additionally, consider seeking out groups with shared interests in games, hobbies, or other pursuits. Each week, it's crucial to break free from the monotony of our daily routines and the hustle and bustle of life to dedicate time to building meaningful relationships. These connections can significantly alleviate feelings of loneliness and depression.

If and when we should feel lonely, there remains an encouraging factor: God sometimes orchestrates events in our lives to intentionally separate us from others, to draw us closer to Himself. It requires trust on our part, acknowledging these times of seclusion are purposely designed to expand our capacity for deeper communion with Him. We must make use of the extra time to immerse our minds in His Word and allow it to fill our hearts with profound meditations. We must open ourselves to the Holy Spirit and permit Him to fill us with God's presence. Then we can find solace in the flood of inspiration His Word brings to our souls and enjoy the boundless grace of God's peace.

Faith flourishes by immersing ourselves in the Holy Bible and living according to its instructions. Our connection to God is strengthened by the sacred Scriptures. As the Holy Bible teaches, God gives grace to the humble and resists the proud.

So, even in moments when God's calling leads you

or me to be alone, we must embrace solitude with a willing heart, knowing His divine plan is at work. For in these seemingly extended periods of solitude, a deeper, more profound relationship with Him awaits. The journey toward understanding His purpose becomes all the more meaningful.

I hope you can submit to Him at the height of loneliness and depression. In His arms, there is companionship, rest, and peace. Trust in Him always, even when it feels like there is no one to trust at all! God *is* good. God is at work. He is faithful, and indeed, all things truly do work together for good to them who love God and who are called according to His purpose, even when God calls us to solitude.

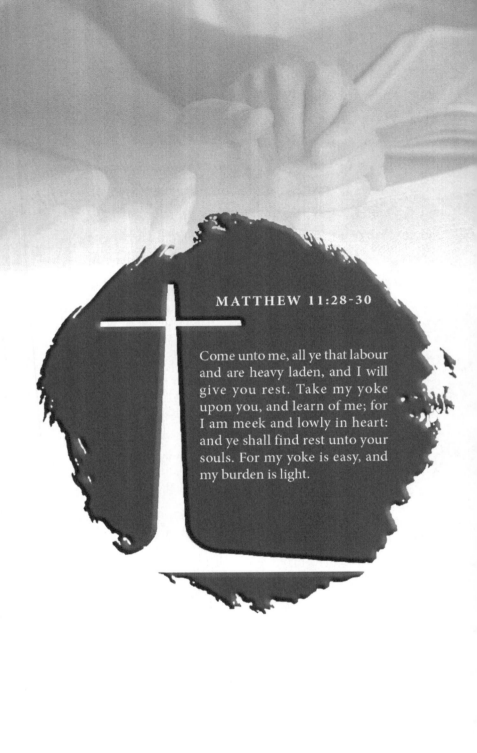

## MATTHEW 11:28-30

Come unto me, all ye that labour and are heavy laden, and I will give you rest. Take my yoke upon you, and learn of me; for I am meek and lowly in heart: and ye shall find rest unto your souls. For my yoke is easy, and my burden is light.

*Have You Considered*

# How Do We Endure Through the Dark of Depression?

WHEN WE ARE CRIPPLED WITH LONELINESS, the urge is to sit or lie down and do nothing. The pain is overwhelming, and the sense of exhaustion is completely debilitating. It takes everything we can do to even get out of bed.

Yet there is power in action and ongoing strength in momentum. God works through obedience, and one of the best ways to obey Him is to find a way to minister, serve, and help others. It will feel completely counterintuitive to do. No one feels lonely and thinks, "I bet serving others will help me feel better." Somehow this is *exactly* how the Holy Spirit works. When we obey Him and take the first heavy steps, the Spirit gives us the ability to keep going. It may not seem like much, but getting out of bed and putting on clothes can be a huge act of obedience to God when our spirits are suffering so much.

This isn't easy. No form of suffering is. But this is one of the most challenging mental blocks to overcome. Loneliness leads directly to depression and despair. It consumes us and tells the lie that things will never change. This is why we can't get out of bed or summon the muscles to brush our teeth. Loneliness crushes us.

But the Lord lifts up those who are weak and exhausted. He renews our strength and breathes life into our beings.

When we pray for His goodness to flow through us, we must take those first steps. Put on a shirt and a pair of pants. Eat a hearty breakfast. Read our Bible and meditate on His Word. Pick up the phone and make a call. Do *something* to get started. We must act in obedience, moving toward others in service and love.

For me, it was calling my pastor friend and asking if I could come over. I had no idea he'd understand what I was going through and his words would give me a glimpse of hope.

When I shared those crazy words, "I am nothingness," my friend looked straight into my eyes and said, "Lawrence, I understand exactly where you are."

Then he briefly opened up about his personal struggles with depression and how he too had experienced the sensation of nothingness that defies explanation. He softly explained, "Depression is not necessarily sin. God sometimes gives, or might we say, He *permits* individuals to go through periods of depression because He is doing an important work in them. He is humbling us down for something good."

Then he encouraged me to remain faithful to the church ministries I was involved in and to continue serving each week. Being occupied with helping others proved to be quite beneficial for me. Engaging in ministry work served as a healthy diversion, steering me away from dwelling too much on my personal distress.

I so appreciated his words, and they reverberated in my mind for many weeks. Ultimately, his words inspired me to study the lives of men and women in the Bible. To my astonishment, I discovered many of God's finest men and women faced depression and despair; some even grappled with suicidal thoughts. Nonetheless, the one who towers over all their testimonies is God. He gave these individuals abundant grace and allowed them to navigate and sometimes wrestle with depression while still finding the strength to serve Him.

Consider Moses' life as an example. Despite experiencing loneliness, depression, and a longing for death at various points in his journey, God used him mightily to deliver a nation of stubborn and rebellious people from slavery, leading them toward the Promised Land. Similarly, Elijah's battle with depression ultimately led to a profound encounter with God; it renewed his zeal to proclaim the truth and confront King Ahab and Queen Jezebel regarding their wicked actions.

Many other biblical accounts of individuals who grappled with depression and despair were Jonah, Peter,

King Hezekiah, King Saul, Judas, Samson, Naomi, Hagar (who was mistakenly judged as intoxicated rather than recognizing her inner struggles), Jeremiah (who faced severe depression due to a surmount of unjust afflictions), Joseph (a teenager) in Genesis, and numerous others who confronted their own emotional turmoil. I am immensely grateful to God that their stories are openly shared in the Bible because their real-life experiences serve as a source of inspiration, showing how we can endure our difficult trials.

In the depths of hopelessness, we can find solace and hope knowing God's transformative presence can dispel even the darkest despair. While we navigate through trials, our faith is refined and our reliance on God deepens. Reflecting on these inspiring examples, we can draw strength and encouragement, recognizing God's unwavering presence in our darkest moments. With His guidance, redemption and triumph can emerge amidst adversity. When we humble ourselves, Christ can be BIG, and as we decrease, He must increase.

I do not comprehend the reasons for my loneliness and why I must endure seasons of depression. I am confident God has a plan. These experiences have gifted me with increased compassion, understanding, and discernment, allowing me to serve God and others more aptly. I have learned the value of withholding judgment and strive to approach every situation with an open heart and mind. Although I never could have predicted my life's path, I am grateful for the blessings which have come from my struggles.

Despite the overwhelming pain and barrenness accompanying my struggles with loneliness and depression, going through these dark times has deepened my appreciation of God's grace, kindness, and love, for He truly loves all of us. I have witnessed miraculous ways God works in our lives. He has brought forth many books out of me to touch countless lives. Moreover, God ingeniously has opened doors for His gospel to be proclaimed in the most unexpected places around the world. I have been blessed to share the message of Jesus Christ—within Buddhist and Hindu temples, public schools, on television in India, and even at a gathering in California sponsored by some enemies of God.

Looking back, I now see during dark periods that God was near and at work in my life. Thankfully, I made a decision not to pursue medical treatment or medication during those periods. In the United States, there is a dangerous tendency to run to medication quickly rather than relying on God. This reliance on pills has become a significant idol that hinders and, in many cases, handicaps the church from truly knowing and experiencing a more profound connection with God.

Moreover, some individuals tend to adopt a perpetual victim mentality, which can be detrimental. While acknowledging we may have been victimized in the past, it's crucial to recognize that we have the power to redefine ourselves in the present. We can choose our identity, especially *in* Christ, and be determined to move forward with goals to accomplish. Personally, I view myself as a conqueror and victor through Christ Jesus. This mindset empowers me to overcome challenges and obstacles that come my way. It enables me to focus on my strengths and abilities rather than dwelling on limitations or past traumas. It isn't easy, and I must admit that I don't know how these words will affect you. But I always want to encourage you to run to Jesus and claim His victory as your own over failures and disappointments.

Sadly, today's prevailing mindset does not prioritize conquering through faith in Christ. Instead, it emphasizes dependence on human interventions and force. We have become averse to any form of discomfort or affliction, resorting to great lengths to avoid them, even if it means resorting to medication. We need to recognize the potential good that can arise from suffering. While I do not oppose the use of medicine and acknowledge God has bestowed upon individuals the ability to treat medical conditions, I firmly believe people would experience more incredible benefits if they allowed God to work through their afflictions, rather than resisting and striving to avoid discomfort and suffering at any cost.

I share these sentiments based on the deep conviction that medication is not the ultimate solution to overcome loneliness and depression. Rather than perceiving depression as an obstacle to be eradicated from my life's journey, I have consciously chosen to embrace its presence. I firmly believe depression is a season of darkness where God invites us to walk alongside Him through the wilderness. And by that, I mean embarking on this journey *together* with God, relying on His guidance and strength through His Word.

Throughout my moments of loneliness and depression, even when I couldn't always sense His presence, He has remained there the whole time. Afterward, when I am out of the dark wilderness, I can look back and see God indeed was very near me.

He is always near, no matter where I am or how I feel.

That is true for me, and it is true for you. God is always near you, no matter where you are or how you feel.

Run to Jesus in your loneliness. Seek His comfort in your depression. Read and meditate on His Word daily. Pray, and then pray some more. Discover His peace by spending time with God.

Then take those first baby steps of obedience so the Holy Spirit can do His mighty work in your life.

**PSALM 23:4**

Yea, though I walk through the valley of the shadow of death, I will fear no evil: for thou art with me; thy rod and thy staff they comfort me.

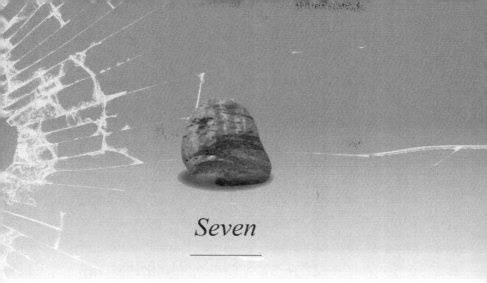

## *Seven*

# DEATH
# A Wolf Returns

MOTHER'S VOICE SHOOK. She could barely form words. I instantly knew something was wrong. My hand trembled as it held the phone.

"Mother?" I said. "What is it? Are you okay?"

I had just made my bed on a balmy summer morning. Today's plan was excellent: We were going to evangelize on the streets of the far East Side of San Diego. Lost people were going to be found. The blind were going to see Jesus!

But my thoughts were interrupted when the phone rang early in the morning. My cell phone had my mother's picture appear when it rang. I answered, expecting some small news or the usual chit-chat we often do during the week. Instead, my mother's tone was unrecognizable; she could barely speak, her sniffling sound crackling on the phone.

"Please," I whispered. "Whatever it is, you can tell me."

"Oh, Lawrence," she struggled to say. "Travis... Travis has died."

A wave of cold bile hit my gut, and I swallowed, feeling like I might throw up. "Wh-what?" I stammered. "I... I didn't hear you quite right, mother... Can you repeat that?"

"Travis is dead, Lawrence. He passed away in the hospital."

I put a hand to my mouth, suddenly sick.

*This can't be real.*

"No, no," I said. "What was he doing in a hospital? I didn't know he was in a hospital!"

Over the phone, I could hear my mother fighting not to break down and sob. "He took... his own life," she managed to say.

At those words, my legs gave out, and I fell to the floor. Not only did I not know he was in a Florida hospital, but I couldn't believe the news that inside a place of medical care, my brother committed suicide.

*No, no. Not my dear brother.*

My phone fell to the floor, bouncing off the carpet.

"Lawrence?" I heard my mother calling through the earpiece. "Are you okay?"

I picked up my phone and started to cry. My mother listened silently on the phone. I managed to whisper a thank you to my mother between sobs. Then I told her I couldn't talk anymore.

"I love you, mother," I said.

I hung up the phone.

All I could do was lay on the floor and cry. Hot blinding tears gushed down my face, and I could do nothing but howl in pain and rage for a long time.

*Why Travis? Why my brother?*

I had no answer. All I knew is someone incredibly close to me was gone, successfully hunted by the enemy. He was dead, and there was nothing more I could do to help him.

MY ABUSER was a sexual deviant. A wolf in human form. He didn't only come for me; he'd manipulated my half-brother, Travis, into many of the same despicable acts too.

Despite its damage to me, the Lord has called me and is continually redeeming me from this trauma. I do not doubt God's Spirit called Travis, too, but I don't know if Travis was willing to answer.

Three days earlier, Travis had been rushed to the hospital for an attempted suicide. They treated his injuries and locked him in the Behavioral Health Unit. After the doctors pumped his stomach of all the many pills he'd taken to end his life, the hospital did not want to provide further care. My brother was eager to get out of the hospital and told a doctor, "I didn't try to kill myself. I was just trying to get high." With these words on paper, the doctors sought to release Travis from their legal care.

But a cousin of mine was at the hospital and intervened on his behalf. My cousin begged the doctors not to release Travis because he told them only what they wanted to hear so he could flee and harm himself again. Unfortunately, on the third day, Travis noticed he wasn't being monitored, and in a desperate act, he used his bed sheet to take his own life.

How could the medical staff be so callous as to disregard the value of a human life? It didn't matter my brother was a drug addict. He was still a human being and deserved to be treated with the same care as a CEO with cancer. If anything, his addiction should have been a red flag that he needed extra care and attention. People who engage in drug abuse and other illicit behaviors silently are crying out for help through their destructive behaviors. Even if these addicts refuse to acknowledge it, their hearts are shattered, and they require unwavering compassion and dedication to be served.

As tears streamed down my face, I sought comfort from my housemate, a beloved friend named Johnny. He heard my cries and came from his room to comfort me. Johnny hugged me and prayed such a beautiful prayer over me, reminding me the Lord is near to those who suffer.

I knew it wasn't God's fault. God is not the author of addiction and self-harm; that's all Satan, and even as I lay on that floor in a swamp of tears, I was furious at the devil. Yes, he won a battle over my brother's earthly life.

But he certainly would not win the war!

Johnny prayed for me again and reassured me the

devil would not emerge victorious. Those words invigorated my heart with a renewed sense of hope. I stood, wiped my cheeks, and released a long sigh. I gazed directly into my friend's eyes and declared, "You're right. Satan is not going to win. And I am going to do something today to make sure of it."

With that, I ran outside to my car, fired up the ignition, and raced across town.

I was in a mood to destroy the enemy. I was sick of his schemes.

It was time to tear down the gates of hell.

TRAVIS WAS MORE than my younger half-brother—he was someone I truly adored.

Our friendship began when we were children, and we always got along well. I fondly remember spending summers playing outside in the countryside at my aunt's home and celebrating his birthdays together in the winters. Later in years as adults, despite living on opposite ends of the United States, Travis and I remained close. While he lived on the East Side and I resided in California, we often spoke on the phone and shared our lives with each other.

Travis had a difficult upbringing beyond his control. When Travis was a young boy, he secretly suffered sexual abuse from the same man as I had. However, the repulsive acts did not arouse his curiosity; instead, they disgusted and sickened him. This burdened him with deep shame and dirty feelings throughout his life. He struggled with doubts about his sexuality, fearing he might be homosexual because of what he was lured into doing. In truth, he had never desired to be with a man that way, and the thought of intimacy with another man repulsed him. But because he had been forced into homosexual acts, he constantly carried a sense of disgust and self-loathing.

To numb the pain, Travis resorted to pills and hooking up with women to deal with his agony. Oh, I wish Travis had embraced more of Jesus Christ's love! Nothing in this world can erase deep-seated shame and deceit except the peace that Christ gives!

To make matters worse for Travis, he suffered further homosexual abuse later in life. His pill addiction led him down some scandalous roads, resulting in numerous stretches of state prison time. During these sentences, he was sexually offended multiple times by fellow inmates with a penchant for sexual violence. The experience pushed him over the edge, feeling utterly filthy and violated. Despite his desperate pleas for help, the correctional officers did nothing to protect him, leaving him vulnerable to repeated acts of cruel and unspeakable violation. The government, medical institutions, and countless others let him down, failing to provide him with the support he desperately needed throughout his life.

Travis didn't want to live like this. He made multiple attempts to overcome his addictions, entering rehab or participating in various treatment and counseling plans.

But for some reason, it never stuck. Travis was easily distracted and fell right back into the wrong crowds and harmful behaviors each time. He often reached out to me, confessing his deep love for Jesus and the Holy Bible, yet feeling like he had lost his way again. He would confide, "I love Jesus, but I can't seem to keep my focus on Him."

One of my favorite memories with Travis occurred during our teenage years. Sitting on the floor together next to my bed in my bedroom, I shared the gospel with him. He expressed his desire to ask Jesus into his heart. Together we prayed, and the joy on his face was evident as he found salvation in Jesus. I'll never forget that moment.

By the time we were young adults, Travis and I had taken considerably different paths in life. At times he seemed to be doing well, living clean, attending a good Bible-preaching church regularly, reading his Bible, and making positive changes. But then I would receive news he had stumbled and was once again involved in pills, partying, and other damaging behaviors.

I prayed incessantly for Travis, seeking God's mercy and grace. I do believe, God answered those prayers.

However, despite the blessings that came his way, Travis remained brokenhearted. Throughout his life, he always had a woman by his side. Yet, his relationships never lasted more than a few years, leaving behind children who were forced to grow up with a missing father. Despite these struggles, Travis continued to cling to relationships with women.

In his last few years of life, my brother appeared

content and happy. He had finally found a woman with whom he expressed true deep love and started a family. He was doing well, staying away from the wrong crowd and not engaging in drug abuse. I often encouraged him on the phone with Bible studies, and he seemed to be redirecting his life toward Jesus Christ. The only concern left was to get married.

However, for reasons no one knows for sure, he began using pills again, inevitably leading him down the wrong path. He grew increasingly unhappy with the way his life was going. Eventually, he took a considerable quantity of pills at once, perhaps more for attention than suicide. Regardless, he could not cope with his deep emotional pain, and his pill addiction failed to provide the relief he needed from years of suffering.

Looking back at Travis' story, all its tragedy, and its brief but remarkable moments of goodness and light, I see a man torn between God's love and the world's claws. Jesus promises to meet us in our suffering, but the father of lies—Satan—says suffering is God's way of punishing us. Rather than meeting us in suffering, God abandons us there—at least according to the liar.

Travis suffered equally as much as I did. He suffered at the hands of a monster.

But when it came time to trust God with those traumas, Travis couldn't bring himself to surrender all. Satan convinced him to trust in pills, women, and a life without commitments. Instead of trusting God with his pain and submitting to His healing ways, Travis relied on the world to make it all better. He bought what Satan sold.

God did not find Travis disgusting or repulsive. God loved him and willingly sent His Son to die for all Travis' sins and reconcile him to a loving Heavenly Father. By the blood of Jesus, Travis was washed clean and robed in the righteousness of the Son of God.

In hindsight, I wish I'd spoken more boldly about Jesus' love when speaking to Travis. I wish I'd devoted more words to our hope in Christ alone and the empty, hollow nature of worldly answers to our pain. I know I tried; I remember speaking passionately about all God was doing in my life.

Sadly, I can't change what happened to Travis. I can only learn from this sad story as I continue to testify to the gospel's truth.

Although Travis' testimony is heart-wrenching, it serves as a warning we should all take to heart. We must be more alert and attentive to people's words and behaviors. We must move beyond superficial interactions and engage in deeper, more meaningful conversations with one another.

Over the years, I have embarked on a personal journey of self-reflection and sought God's guidance to help me become more open and authentic with others. I have had to learn to forgive myself, my brother Travis, and all the individuals who failed him. Accepting God's sovereignty has enabled me to move forward with His plan for my life.

Suffering is solitary. When we share our grief with others, it helps us to adjust to our loss. In the wake of Travis' passing, my heart was shattered, yet God has been faithful in healing my soul. I have witnessed how Travis' death has become a source of inspiration for many people. I have been able to identify some individuals who are struggling with suicidal thoughts. I extend a compassionate ear to listen to their stories, share Travis' testimony, give them hugs, and offer words of encouragement. I find immense joy in rescuing them from the deceptive grip of suicide as a viable solution. Instead, I can lead them to Jesus Christ, offer friendship, and provide resources to help them cope with their struggles and find the healing they need.

But before I would learn all this and process the full extent of my fury at Satan for what he had done, I was on a mission.

And driving like a madman across San Diego, I just needed to arrive safely to carry it out.

I HAD A PLAN. I had been assisting a church on the east side of town with outreach programs to raise awareness about their daily tent revival services.

Upon my arrival at the site, a team of two pastors and church members were waiting to greet me. They were informed of my brother's passing. One of them, Ernie, had been told by my pastor and was ready to accompany me throughout the day. Everyone present offered me heartfelt embraces and comforting words. One of the pastors told me I did not need to work if I didn't feel up to it.

I felt more than up to it. It was time for payback.

After praying with Ernie, we set off to a nearby neighborhood to invite people to the tent revival. We and a third young guy walked down the street, passing out flyers and sharing the event details with everyone we encountered.

I balled my fists and glared, ready to strike at the first sign of Satan's influence.

The first man I encountered on the street was a young, white skater-type guy, around 22 years old, wearing a black shirt, blue jeans, and slightly overweight. Usually, I would make small talk to smooth the conversation out, but in my current state, I was not myself.

"I want to invite you to hear the gospel at our tent revival tonight," I blurted, extending a pamphlet toward him.

He glanced at my hand and snorted. "Buddy, I don't want anything to do with God," he said.

Then he turned to walk away.

Before I continue, allow me to offer a word of caution against acting on emotions as you read further. Sharing Christ's gospel necessitates a mindset beyond satisfying personal desires. We must not let our emotions sway us when encountering rejection of God's message. It's God they are rejecting, not us. Our commitment to sharing the gospel must be rooted in obedience to Christ's Great Commission rather than driven by results.

But this time, I wasn't having it. I was sick of Satan's sway.

Staring at the young man, I quickly retorted, "That's

ridiculous. Don't you realize you're about to die and go to hell, and God is trying to reach out to you before you die?"

As the words left my lips, an intense emotion swept over me. Had I just prophesied? Or was I merely a raging, emotional basket case about to get stabbed on the street?

The man turned around. His face was dark, his eyes narrow. "You can't judge me," he growled.

"I'm not judging you," I answered. "You don't want anything to do with God, but when you get to hell, you won't be able to blame Him. God desires to save you, but you don't want anything to do with Jesus, who shed His blood for you."

He held up his hands to shush me, saying, "Woe, buddy," but before he could continue, I cut him off and yelled, "My younger brother just died!"

The words cut through the air like a sword. The man's mouth opened, but no words came out.

"It's true!" I continued. "This morning, he thought he had another fifty years of life. But right now, he is in eternity. You probably think you will live another fifty years, too. But maybe you will die today, just like my brother. And if you die, you *will* go straight to hell."

The man's face softened as he heard my words. His eyes danced around for a moment as if he was trying to think of a sharp response. But when he spoke again, his tone was gentle.

"Man, I'm sorry to hear about your brother," he said. "Don't feel sorry for me," I said. "Feel sorry for yourself.

Because if you don't realize you're a sinner in need

of a Saviour, you're the one to be pitied."

I stopped, my chest heaving from lack of breathing during my testimony. The man stared back at me, his eyes narrowing again. But the softness remained, his face heavy with thought.

"You're some street preacher," he muttered.

"I'm not a preacher," I said. "I'm just a sinner like you, but saved by God. And I'm sick and tired of Satan deceiving people like you on the way to hell."

He opened his mouth to speak but must have thought better of it. Then he took the pamphlet from my hand.

"Okay," he said quietly, studying the cover. "Maybe this is what I need to hear today."

"Yes, you do."

He exhaled, his shoulders sagging. "You're right, man," he said. "I do need to be saved. Seriously, I've never thought about it the way you put it. To tell the truth, this is exactly what I needed to hear."

When I heard that, my spirit instantly calmed down. I continued to listen as he asked, "I've heard about Jesus. And I know He died and rose from the grave, but how do I get saved?"

As I regained normal breathing, I tried to restrain my ecstatic joy at his softening spirit that had miraculously become open to listening. Over the next fifteen minutes, I sat side-by-side with this man on a curb, opened my compact Bible, and read from God's Word exactly how to be saved. A profound beauty enveloped the moment when he humbly lowered his head on the street. He confessed his sins to the Lord Jesus and prayed to God to save him.

Despite my overly aggressive and dogmatic demeanor, God's powerful truth brought this man to Jesus Christ's saving grace. I hadn't torn down all the pillars of hell, but I'd thrown a rock through one of its windows.

Yes, Travis was gone. I still weep at the thought and miss him dearly.

But God uses all things for the good of those who love Him. Even the death of those we hold dearest.

While the wolf may win many battles, it will not win the war!

## 2 CORINTHIANS 4:8-9

We are troubled on every side, yet
not distressed; we are perplexed,
but not in despair; Persecuted,
but not forsaken; cast down, but
not destroyed;

## *Have You Considered*

---

# Why Does God Continue to Let Satan Have His Way?

D O YOU EVER FEEL HOPELESS? If you've ever lost a cherished loved one like I did, someone similar to Travis, then you can certainly relate to my feelings of utter hopelessness and despair.

Or do you ever feel your life is pointless or your situation won't improve no matter what you do? In these moments, we often ask, "What's the point?" with a sarcastic drawl.

If this is you, I hear you and understand something of what your pain is like!

I received a tangible reminder from God that even in the midst of seemingly hopeless situations, there is always a renewed dawn of hope after prolonged periods of darkness.

Recently after a ten-day trip to the United States,

my heart sank when I returned home to El Salvador. I love gardening, and I've been tending a beautiful hibiscus bush outside my apartment. When I returned after two weeks, the once-thriving plant bundle of life was nearly dead. Withered and dried up, there were no signs of life.

Despite my sadness, I decided to take action by providing it with plant food and consistent watering. I had to put in a lot of work, but on day seven, it began to sprout new baby leaves. A month later, the bush was flourishing again with an abundance of beautiful blossoms and fresh green leaves.

This simple experience was a powerful reminder that even when circumstances seem bleak and hopeless, God always offers renewed hope for tomorrow's future.

We all encounter moments when our journey leads us through the wilderness. These circumstances can be disheartening, particularly when the light ahead seems obscured. Feeling lost and uncertain, we may be unsure of how to move forward. It's important to recognize we won't always walk through refreshing valleys or triumphant mountaintops. Nevertheless, amid the challenges, we can find comfort in knowing each new day presents opportunities for fulfillment. As we journey forward, we will forge new friendships, achieve new milestones, and experience inner peace, all with a resounding sense of purpose and meaning in life.

The process of overcoming hopelessness is not a passive one; serendipity does not occur on its own. While we can pray to God for miracles and deliverance, we must remember these are not mystical events that happen in the ether. God's involvement always responds to our efforts, manifesting through actions that align with His perfect will and His permissive will. When we take action, God responds in kind; He is actively present in our physical world, guiding and unfolding His divine plan through our choices and the paths we choose.

To that end, certain practices and habits help me persevere through suffering, especially in times of hopelessness and despair. These simple but essential behaviors take time to develop into character traits. If you can begin practicing them now and making them a part of your daily routine, I promise you will begin to discern the gentle, whispering voice of God more clearly. Jesus Christ will become more of the preeminence in your life.

1. Be faithful daily to make time to praise God.

Praising God is of utmost importance, as it cultivates our hearts with gratitude for both the blessings we have as well as the things withheld from us. We don't always require everything we desire. When I speak about praise, I'm referring to the practice of expressing gratitude for specific blessings or aspects of life. For instance, giving thanks to God for the small blessings, like the ability to use our fingernails to pick up papers, and for the grandeur gifts like our home, job, and a sound mind. Praise dispels doubts, lies, and ingratitude in our hearts, dissipating bitterness and anger lingering from past troubles. Engaging in daily worship allows us to embrace clarity, joy, and freedom in God's presence, reminding us of our dependence on Him.

2. Be faithful daily to read and meditate on God's Holy Bible.

God's Word nourishes our spirits, imparting invaluable wisdom, understanding, and knowledge. As we immerse ourselves in this practice, we experience transformation, finding guidance and strength to persevere through life's challenges. Setting aside dedicated time each day enables us to tune out worldly distractions and engage in quiet communion with God. Within the scriptures, we actively need to seek Christ, asking the Holy Spirit questions and reflecting on the passages' meaning and application. This intentional pursuit of God through His Word brings profound and lasting benefits to our lives, empowering us to navigate victoriously through whatever troubles come along our journey.

3. Be faithful to often commune with God in prayer.

God reveals Himself to us through prayer, where His presence becomes palpable. Prayer deepens our communion with the Father. It strengthens our faith and shields us from pitfalls of undue self-reliance, anchoring us firmly in reliance upon God. Just as Jesus turned to prayer daily, we, too, discover a wellspring of comfort, direction, and profound closeness with the Father. Likewise, it is imperative we embrace this cherished privilege to engage with God regularly, maintaining an ongoing communion that steers our thoughts and actions as well as gracefully accompanies us throughout each moment of our journey in life.

4. Be faithful to church and God's family.

Make it a priority to attend regularly and actively

serve in a local church that prioritizes preaching the Holy Bible, evangelizing, and emphasizing the Lord Jesus Christ. In today's contemporary world where many churches have apostatized away from the Holy Bible, finding a congregation that exalts Christ in faithful preaching and teaching of His Bible is becoming increasingly imperative.

It is essential to surround ourselves with fellow Christians who hunger for God, desire to exalt Christ and see others saved and discipled. While all congregations consist of individuals at different levels of spiritual maturity, this diversity is beneficial.

It fosters godly personal character, such as patience and temperance; and being in the company of spiritually healthy Christians motivates us to deepen our discipleship and strive to become more like Christ. This supportive community provides an environment filled with love, care, and encouragement. Together, we can stir up our spiritual gifts, support one another, and bear each other's burdens, all while edifying fellow believers and reaching the world for Christ.

5. Be faithfully involved in purposeful ministry.

Regularly volunteer to step out of your comfort zone and serve the "least of these" around whom you are least comfortable. We need to weekly schedule times to serve others in various ways: To evangelize. To disciple. To encourage the brokenhearted. To feed the poor. To serve the downtrodden.

Life's purpose extends beyond ourselves. Life is more than just about *me*. Life is about God and others. Engaging in ministry helps us shift our focus away from ourselves and direct it toward God and others in need.

Once you begin to minister to someone else, your own problems and pains fade into the background. You are reminded that many others are enduring worse suffering than you are. With this awareness, you'll find joy. The joy you experience through ministry will endure long after the act itself, as you'll come to recognize ministry is not necessarily only for the person you are serving; it's also for your own well-being—because it is you who needs help.

There have been moments when I have felt discouraged, lonely, and down in the dumps. Despite these negative emotions, I still put on my shoes, grabbed a bunch of gospel tracts, and went out on the streets to minister. I didn't feel like ministering at first; however, I knew by reaching out to someone who needed to hear about Jesus or encouragement and prayer, all my discouragement and negative emotions would melt away. Ministry acts as a healing balm, redirecting our focus towards Jesus Christ, for in Him is access to true freedom and fulfillment.

6. Be faithful to cheerfully give God your tithes and offerings each week.

You may wonder: How do tithing and giving offerings contribute to the alleviation of my suffering? Doing so is an act of obedience to God that goes beyond mere financial transactions. Regularly giving each week becomes a powerful tool for alleviating the suffering embedded within our spirits. The act of willingly giving something that holds deep personal value, money, accompanied by cheerfulness and gratitude, has a transformative effect on us. Giving extends beyond the boundaries of self-centered concerns, propelling us into a mindset that fosters well-being, nurtures confidence in God, and enriches us with peace. We discover that giving is its own reward, unveiling a valuable and wholesome practice that benefits both those who give and those who receive.

WE KNOW THESE BEHAVIORS LEAD to godliness because they are the character traits of Jesus Christ. He suffered temptation and pain just like us, and He practiced a lifestyle that put faith in the Father above all else. He prayed and studied His Father's scriptures; attended synagogue and fellowshipped with followers of God; and spent His life serving the weak, lost, and outcast, reconciling them to the Father.

It is possible to regain hope, even from the deepest pit of despair. When we adopt Christlike character traits, they become a regular practice—a lifestyle. We can even regain hope when we are the culprits behind our own demise. During tough times, we are vulnerable to making wrong decisions and often engage in self-destructive behavior patterns that lead toward our own undoing. In these situations, we may feel like we've lost everything—people may leave us, forsake us, and want nothing to do with us anymore. But even in the darkest moments, we must continue moving forward. We must trust that following the example of Christ's actions will guide us toward a closer intimacy with God and away from the deceitful entanglements of Satan's worldly web of lies. Therefore, commit yourself to this pursuit and persist with patience and determination.

You may also need to make tangible changes to your situation, whether that's changing your career, a new passion, new friends, or changing your location. Seek help from friends, pastors, or counselors to change your habits and routines positively. Finally, focus on ways to cultivate hope and move towards a more positive future. That way, even when everything seems lost, you'll be able to remember there's always a way forward.

With Jesus, there is always hope. That hope is for us now on this broken Earth and later when we are taken Home to be with our Father in Heaven.

Don't let the father of lies con you into believing all is lost. With Christ, all is *never* lost.

Jesus is the finder of His sheep, even the one that leaves the ninety-nine. Lean on Him and trust in His ways; you'll always have light to guide you through the darkness.

**PROVERBS 3:5-6**

Trust in the LORD with all thin
heart; and lean not unto thine
own understanding. In all thy
ways acknowledge him, and he
shall direct thy paths.

## *Eight*

---

# ANGER
# Damned Justice

"I CAN'T ACCEPT THESE!" Normally I try not to raise my voice. I don't like yelling.

But now I was screaming, and I didn't feel the least bit bad about it.

The photographer simply crossed his arms and pointed at the pile of photos I'd hired him to take. "Well, I'm not keeping them," he said. "They're yours now."

"These aren't the sizes I asked for!" I countered. "You need to print new ones for me."

He shook his head. "I don't know what you're talking about. This is what we agreed to in our contract."

"The hell we did," I hollered.

Then I realized a fateful thing: *I'd left the contract at my house.*

"No, you didn't," the photographer sneered. "Now take these and leave."

"No!" I cried. "You lied to me, and now I don't the have photographs I need for my business project this week. Why won't you help me?"

"Look, it's not my problem," he retorted. "You changed your mind, not me."

"Give me my money back!" I yelled.

He scowled as if I was a lunatic. "No."

"You're cheating me! Pay me back!"

"No."

My anger was uncontrollably erupting. I couldn't hold it in any longer. My eyes locked onto a crystal vase on the table before us, its hue a glossy mixture of grey and white. Without any moment of thought, I reached for the vase and lifted it into the air.

"You—will—*pay me!*" I bellowed.

Then I hurled the vase to the floor. It burst into an ear-splitting crash, sending shiny shards flying in every direction.

"That's it," the photographer said, flying off his chair. "I'm calling the cops, you freaking psycho!"

My entire body was shaking, jolted by what I'd just done. The image of blue-clad officers storming the room flew through my brain.

*Oh no, you're not,* I thought.

So I stood up and turned to leave. I had to get out no matter what.

"Where are you going?" He called after me. "Hey!"

I kept walking.

Then he said something I'll never forget: "You know, your mom is still here!"

I froze.

I had completely forgotten the person who had come with me. I'd told her it would be a quick and easy pickup, and then we'd head out to lunch.

*I'd just destroyed that vase in front of my mother.*

I stopped and turned around. I could hear her soft, sweet voice trying to reason with the photographer, begging him not to call the police; earnestly working to smooth it all over, saying I wasn't being myself. The sound of her voice sent a chill up my body.

"Let's go, mother," I said.

But I couldn't bear to look her in the eyes. The sheer shame of it would crush me.

So I marched through the studio and out the door, and the image of the shattered crystal burned into my mind.

ANGER IS A WEED with deep roots. It doesn't magically or suddenly appear, though its arrival may be sudden and surprising.

Anger is a complicated sin to dislodge from our hearts because, much like an infested garden, it is inextricably woven among the plants supposed to be there. It blends in with the rest and escapes scrutiny by blooming its own flora.

Then the day comes when the flowers begin to die, choked and harassed by the pervasive weeds. I had let my anger overrun the garden of my heart, and now I couldn't hold it back any longer.

Suffice it to say, the rest of that day with my mother was ruined. She wanted to talk to me about my outburst, but I didn't want to hear about it. I couldn't imagine her shock at witnessing my actions and her horror at my unwillingness to discuss them.

However, the day after, my mother sat me down and insisted that we talk about it. She voiced her concern about my anger and urged me to surrender it to the Lord. This incident was the first time she witnessed me act out in such an aggressive manner. She was taken aback and frightened I could end up hurting someone.

Yet I still didn't want to admit I was in the wrong. "You're shaking, Lawrence," she told me during the conversation. "Even listening to me is making you angry all over again!" Mother was right: I was still livid at the photographer, her, and myself. I was furious with everyone involved and ultimately at God for not making situations turn out the way I wanted them to in the first place.

While we both were shocked by the situation, I privately knew this wasn't the first time I had acted out this way. It was becoming a new norm for me to lash out, throw things, and give people a piece of my mind. But doing so in front of my mother was more embarrassing than I could imagine. For the first time in a while, I felt palpable shame at my anger and that I had allowed it to escalate to such a point. Before, I could hide my rage; this time, I couldn't, and it was no longer a secret sin I could control. All I wanted to do was walk away and die.

Where did this aggressive rage come from?

And why was it leading to such abusive behavior, even in front of my beloved mother?

IN MY HIGH SCHOOL AND COLLEGE YEARS, there was a deep-seated anger growing within me. I was oblivious to it, often thinking this kind of anger was reserved for the most violent offenders among us. Either I didn't exhibit signs of this anger yet, or I was completely blind to them. Nonetheless, as I entered my early twenties and moved across the country to San Diego on my own, it began to manifest itself more prominently as I more often raised my tone to let others know just how angry their actions made me.

Upon completing my college education, I relocated to the gorgeous city of San Diego in sunny Southern California, where pristine beaches and palm trees abound, making it feel like a slice of paradise on earth. However, in the first year of living alone and away from my loved ones, I began to notice my sudden outbursts of uncontrollable anger. It frightened me tremendously, and I couldn't comprehend its origin. The anger terrified me; it was as if a second person lived in me, a Mr. Hyde who could hurt anyone who dared cross him. I also didn't have any close trusted friends to confide in, and I found myself getting agitated easily and sometimes infuriated over even the most trivial matters.

Like any sensible person, I attempted to mask my fury in the presence of others. The threat of public shame is enough to make most people behave. But once alone at home, I would scream, cuss, and shout at the emptiness. Sometimes I would throw things or even damage property, such as punching a hole in a wall or slamming kitchen plates on the floor. Clearly, I wasn't in control of my anger; I was merely hiding it to avoid looking bad in front of others.

This kind of fear is incredibly dangerous because it leads to a false sense of self-discipline. When we are able to corral our sin and keep it locked away from others, we are tricked into perceiving ourselves as virtuous. But the Apostle Paul knows exactly what this behavior is, and he wrote about it in his second letter to the church in Corinth.

"For though I made you sorry with a letter, I do not repent, though I did repent: for I perceive that the same epistle hath made you sorry, though it were but for a season," he said, referring to the firm language he was compelled to use regarding sexual sin in the book of First Corinthians. "Now I rejoice," he continued, "not that ye were made sorry, but that ye sorrowed to repentance: for ye were made sorry after a godly manner, that ye might receive damage by us in nothing. For godly sorrow worketh repentance to salvation not to be repented of: *but the sorrow of the world worketh death*" (2 Corinthians 7:8-10, emphasis added).

As I became aware of my anger, I primarily felt "sorrow of the world," meaning fear of embarrassment or worldly loss. I worried I'd lose out on earthly goods like relationships, job opportunities, or even my legal freedoms. But my heart wasn't ready to embrace the "godly sorrow" that would lead me toward repentance.

That "sorrow of the world" peaked when I exploded before my mother. Perhaps the deepest shame I could feel was the sting of her rebuke. But when she sat me down and spoke candidly that I needed to repent of my anger, I wanted to fight back. I was a grown man. How dare she tell me how to feel when I had been wronged and unfairly treated!

My anger didn't spare even her, the most beloved person in my life. She relished visiting me in San Diego, and I always eagerly anticipated her visits. We explored many breathtaking sights and created fond memories together. We indeed had a blast together during her trips. However, on some occasions, I became agitated with my mother. It was more than just showing disrespect in her presence. I would inexplicably sigh around her, argue over trivial matters, and even experience fits of rage. She recognized I had an anger issue and encouraged me to get some help, such as counseling or a class to teach me how to manage my negative emotions. When my mother tried to advise me, I became defensive and argued, reluctant to believe or accept her reproof. Instead of listening to her wise counsel, I often let out deep sighs of frustration and walked away.

One evening, after years of struggling with my anger, I hit a breaking point. I was alone; I threw myself to the floor, lying on the living room carpet, crying and pouring out my anger to God in a vehement prayer. Though I still didn't understand everything about my anger, I vividly remember that night I was particularly upset about sexual abuse. I kept asking God, "Why? Why! Why did You let this happen to me?"

God seemed unresponsive. The room was dark and quiet, and I kept weeping and crying out to Him for a long time. But after pouring out my anger to God for an hour, exhaustion overcame me, and I found myself lying on the floor quietly sobbing. Suddenly to my surprise, I heard God's voice within my heart. It was not a normal human voice, yet it was clear as day, and it softly resounded deep within me.

The voice said, "'Why' is not the question."

God's voice within me took me aback. My faith was weak then, and I was not accustomed to hearing God. However, I knew without a doubt God had spoken to me. It was indeed someone else's voice that was not mine. His simple statement resonated deeply within me, and I immediately stopped crying, sat up, and found the means to calm myself down.

As I sat in stillness before God, His words began to make sense. Perhaps I *had* been asking God the wrong question. With a clear mind and a lifted heart, I asked, "What am I supposed to do? What do You want, Lord?"

At that very moment, on my living room floor, I

experienced an indescribable and profound transformation. Even now, I remain in awe, still trying to grasp how God worked His wonders. Words fail to capture the depth and magnitude of my experience, but without a doubt, the impossible became possible solely by God's might. Suddenly, I felt the mass of anger that had consumed me for so long literally pulled upward off of me as if lifted by a strong hand. A tremendous weight was removed from my chest and shoulders. A sense of lightness and peace enveloped me. As I inhaled, the air felt fresh, sweet, and crisp, unlike so many anxious breaths I had taken in the last few years. The anger that had held me captive vanished, and I felt like a renewed person. At that moment, I could feel God's immense love embracing me.

That night, I slept soundly and rested perfectly.

GOD DOESN'T ALWAYS heal our sins this way. God is infinitely wise. He often allows us to struggle with issues much longer, forcing us to depend on Him like never before. I certainly hope when you call out to God for forgiveness and cleansing, the Lord takes your struggle with sin away as He did with my anger. But if He doesn't, I pray you trust Him and believe He can and will heal you, whatever brings Christ the greatest honor.

As I've mentioned before, I love gardening and I view it as a metaphor for our hearts. Gardens are meant to produce fruit, just like our hearts. If our hearts are gardens intended to produce good fruit, a Master Gardener must carefully remove the weeds. My anger was a network of weeds that had grown thick and full for many years. Removing them wasn't going to be a quick, one-day operation. Yes, God pulled my anger out of me in an instant, however, it took years of prayer and pleading, of regularly reaching out and begging Jesus to be Lord of my heart, for the anger to leave me. And more, I'm still not completely free of this sin, as I am simply a mortal man living under the shadow of Satan's present dominion. I still find myself tempted to get frustrated and bothered when the nuisances of life disrupt my plans.

But I'll never forget how God took away that weight of anger from me because I know right where it went: to the hands and feet of Jesus on the cross. These are the very burdens Christ carried for our sake. He bears our sins in the holes wrought by the cruel nails. As Isaiah prophesied so long ago, "Surely he hath borne our griefs, and carried our sorrows: yet we did esteem him stricken, smitten of God, and afflicted" (Isaiah 53:4).

It doesn't matter how thick the weeds are in your heart; it doesn't matter how deep their roots penetrate. The Lord can deal with them. He is the Master Gardener and the deliverer of good fruit. He took anger from me so I didn't have to carry the weight of rage against my abuser anymore. He took it and now happily carries that burden for me.

Now He is ready to carry your burden for you.

The question is whether or not you'll trust Jesus to do so.

**GALATIANS 2:20**

I am crucified with Christ: nevertheless I live; yet not I, but Christ liveth in me: and the life which I now live in the flesh I live by the faith of the Son of God, who loved me, and gave himself for me.

## *Have You Considered*

# The Real Reason We Struggle with Anger?

D O YOU ANGER EASILY? Do you wish others would stop being so foolish, annoying, or non-compliant?

Not long after God healed my anger, I met a man who spoke some simple but profound words that changed my perspective on the matter. During a short time together in a business matter, neither of us said much of anything, but oddly when he did speak, he softly said, "Anger is never the problem."

"What do you mean?" I asked.

"Anger is a symptom of a deeper root issue," he calmly replied—and after a moment, he continued, "and that's the *true* problem." And he never said another word.

His remark about anger lingered in my mind for the rest of the evening. When I returned home, I immediately spent the next few hours poring over a Bible Concordance and reading every verse related to "anger."

It was quite a task that took a week to study, as there are over 400 such verses. But after carefully taking notes and compiling a comprehensive summary of my findings, I realized something incredible: Unrighteous anger always stems from pride. Yes, it is often triggered by injustice (like my abuse), but what transforms grief into anger is pride.

I would regularly get upset when people didn't behave or speak in a way that aligned with my expectations. As a well-disciplined young adult and a passionate advocate for justice, I had developed a rigid code that I expected everyone else to adhere to, given what had happened to me.

Technically there was nothing wrong with the principles I espoused. Nevertheless, my merciless way of enforcing them on others was terribly wrong and gravely unjust. Whatever evil had been done to me did not justify my passing on the burden of shame to others. I needed to take my grief and outrage to one person: the Lord Jesus. No one else is equipped to handle it, nor can anyone else bear such a burden. It's not fair Jesus Christ died for transgressions; however, it's the way God lovingly chose to reconcile us to Him.

Anger is the result of the world refusing to meet our desires. We want God-level power without God-level sacrifice.

The Apostle James provided valuable insight into the dangers of unchecked desires. In his epistle, James wrote, "But every man is tempted, when he is drawn away of his own lust, and enticed. Then when lust hath conceived, it bringeth forth sin: and sin, when it is finished, bringeth forth death" (James 1:14-15).

I noticed this passage warns when our own lustful desires entice us, they will lead us down a destructive path toward sin and, ultimately, death. Many desires begin innocently and seem reasonable, but when tainted with selfish ambitions, they become sinful. This passage is a powerful reminder to be mindful of our desires and ensure they align with God's will for our lives.

To put James' passage in the form of a flow chart:

DESIRE → SELFISHNESS → TEMPTATION → ACTION → DEATH
(SIN)

By God's mercy, this death is not irreparable, as Christ's blood is sufficient to pay the total price of our sins, no matter how many or foul. When we repent of our selfish desires and ways, God is faithful to forgive and cleanse us of these blemishes.

Like all sin, anger does not exist in isolation; external influences can subtly trigger it. Satan exploits these triggers to remind us of our pain and fears, luring us into patterns of sin. To counter this, we must identify our sin triggers and establish systems of repentance and accountability to resist their influence. The enemy must be treated as such—an adversary to be confronted with determination. Invest time to meditate and study scriptures, pray, and fellowship with other believers so you can uncover your sin triggers and earnestly seek healing from God in those areas.

Over the years, God has put me in uncomfortable situations to confront and discuss my past. Yet, in the process, God has taught me how to steer away from anger and accept what He allows to occur. Through His guidance, I've learned some wisdom on how to channel negative energy into productive and positive actions and thoughts. It takes a lot of courage to face our past, but with God's help, we can turn our painful experiences into something meaningful and transformative. I am grateful for the wisdom and strength God gives me. I pray to continue to grow and learn from Him as I move forward on my journey.

I hope you find a piece of that wisdom as you wrestle with your own anger and frustrations and learn to entrust them to the Lord!

**PSALM 119:71**

It is good for me that I have been afflicted; that I might learn thy statutes.

*Nine*

# JUDGMENT
## Satan's Great Divider

I EXPECTED IT TO BE BAD. But I had no idea it would be *this* bad. Texts came in day and night. The phone rang unusually more.

Knowing the reason for each, I'd take a deep breath and whisper a quick prayer for patience and strength.

Then I'd pick up my phone.

Someone I had known for a long time would be on the other end of the line when I answered. Pastors. Fellow missionaries. A distant cousin. Dear friends. Family.

"Hi," I'd say, attempting to sound like I didn't know what the call was about.

Sometimes I'd be answered by silence, the hiss and crackle of a dormant phone line. Other times they'd abruptly start bluntly talking to me in a condescending manner.

The worst was the broken, pitiful voice some had when they asked, "Is it true?"

"Yes," I answered each time. "It is true."

Some dear friends communicated grievous words directly at me. They said I was all kinds of things I wasn't. One more or less called me a pedophile to my face, a truly terrible insult given my past. And another called me a coward.

But I sat there and took it. It was the only way to possibly save these relationships. If I believed the gospel—I did then, and I do now—I had to trust in God's promises.

When they were done, I wiped my tears and tried to end the conversation on good terms. "I'm sincerely sorry this hurts you so much," I told each person. "I hope you can forgive me."

Some people refused to forgive. At least, that's what I believe because they totally shunned me out of their lives.

On different occasions, some friends conveyed their sentiments they never wanted to see or talk to me again, sharing this devastating news through text, phone calls, or to my face on various occasions. Others simply ignored me and never answered my calls.

Still, I extended kindness. I didn't want events to go this way. Yes, I had sinned, but I had repented. My repentance was constant, an ongoing dialogue of sincere prayer between me and the Lord. It was a public matter now. So many people knew of my sins, and many seemed to feel they had the right to talk to me about it.

I kept trying to heal, praying for reconciliation and

healing for those I had disappointed and hurt.

Some people far in between desired such reconciliation, but many threw their Christlikeness aside and abhorred me.

Wasn't I following the path of the gospel? Hadn't I obeyed my Heavenly Father, confessed my sins, and sought to turn from them?

Apparently, it didn't matter. My sins were too egregious for some people.

In those days, I learned one of the most terrible and painful lessons: To be judged and publicly slandered is perhaps the worst punishment and pain of all.

And the people who did it to me claim to call Jesus Christ Lord.

What went wrong?

Why were my friends and closest companions suddenly throwing me to the wolves?

I ACCEPTED JESUS' invitation to be my Saviour as a teenager on February 18, 1995. However, the fact that I placed my faith in the Lord Jesus Christ for salvation did not mean all my pains, bewilderment, and allurements suddenly vanished. They were still present in me then and now, as they are in everyone walking among the living.

When my abuser took advantage of me, his behavior rewired my natural desires and twisted them against God's loving design. He allured my passions to seek pleasure and peace in the arms of other men. He had tricked me into thinking our time together was a place of acceptance. I'm not surprised his wicked schemes affected me the way they did.

For many years I had no idea where my same-sex attraction originated. Still, when I reached college and specific memories became more apparent, I began to put the pieces together. The abuse was an obvious answer to the question, but another event also had a profound effect.

When I was five years old (around the same time my abuser entered the picture), I visited a friend's house. At the time, he was six, and I had no idea his teenage sister was sexually abusing *him!* Neither of us understood what that was or what it meant, but it was happening all the same. Playing outside together, as kids frequently do, we snuck into a neighbor's garage when she wasn't home and found a set of discarded couch cushions on the floor. I remember cotton puffs spilling out of rips in the fabric like toxic yellow storm clouds.

My friend offered to show me something cool. Like any good friend, I told him I was up for it. So he told me to lay down on the cushions and then mimed sexual actions with me and my clothed body. Writing this now (and no doubt as you read it), bile rushes up my esophagus at the thought of little boys doing such inappropriate things. But at the time, blind in my naivety, I found it fun, like a variation on wrestling or even tag. A small voice cried out in my gut, telling me something about it wasn't right. But I was having fun, and nothing in my friend's behavior seemed insidious— after all, he was only doing what his older sister had shown him. Within a few minutes, we grew bored of this "game," ran out of the garage, and I never saw the inside again.

At this moment, we see Satan's corrupting power. In the guise of innocence, Satan takes something beautiful, the intimacy to be shared between a married man and wife, and eviscerates it. Physical touch between friends is a good thing, a gift that strengthens healthy bonds. But Satan perverted my definition of male-to-male contact and associated it with sex and sexuality. I was far too young even to grasp what sex was. It seemed like a game as hide-and-seek. From those days onward, my psyche was drawn toward other men for the consummation and completion I was designed to seek in a female bride.

Of course, some will say I'm lying to myself. Why fight against "who I am" when I could live a happy life as an "out" homosexual man?

For one, I don't find "who I am" in my sexuality but in Christ Jesus and His Holy Bible. I find who I am in God's divine design, not Satan's fallen corruption.

Second, I don't believe I've been attracted to other men because I was born homosexual or that my attraction, wherever it came from, needs to be justified through a twisted interpretation of Scripture. I know what God intended when he created Adam and Eve; I also understand what He provided when He wed His Son Jesus to the Church, illustrating the beauty of marriage. Both of these relationships, one biological and the other spiritual, point to deliberately crafted heterosexual, two-gender union. I am and always will be on board with this vital doctrine of Scripture and God's design, and it is my prayer God heals my same-sex attraction so I can enjoy the fruit of His blessed design.

Amid all my searching for answers, God never stopped pursuing me, and His love keeps me in a productive struggle against temptation and sin.

Does that mean I never find myself attracted to men? Hardly. I'm aware I will probably struggle with this for the rest of my life. But this makes me like everyone else.

"For all have sinned, and come short of the glory of God," Paul wrote in his letter to the Romans, "being justified freely by his grace through the redemption that is in Christ Jesus: Whom God hath set forth to be a propitiation through faith in his blood, to declare his righteousness for the remission of sins that are past, through the forbearance of God" (Romans 3:23-25).

As I've admitted throughout this book, I struggle with numerous sins, not just same-sex attraction. We recently explored my anger and pride; in a few pages, we'll see how quick I was to chase worldly wealth instead of God's Kingdom. One of my notable sins is my unwillingness to forgive others. Yet Jesus teaches me to "forgive...every one his brother their trespasses," as revenge is the Lord's to handle, not mine (Matthew 18:35).

My life is rife with sin, but all so God's mercy and grace can abound. Yet none of these sins has garnered a reaction from others like when I let myself believe the insecurities in my mind and acted on same-sex attraction. I can admit this hurt several people close to me. Many felt misled and even betrayed, as I had tried to keep this part of me a secret before all who knew me.

But people weren't calling me confrontationally because they found out I'd broken a vase in a photographer's studio. They didn't blow up my phone with questions because I'd disrespected my mother. And they certainly didn't spread gossip about me and slander my name to the world because I owned a nice home and didn't give that money to the poor.

I was slandered because I had committed a particular kind of sin that causes Christians to lose their heads. I had committed *homosexual* sins, and in this day and age, it doesn't seem to matter how much one repents. I became an instant outcast, and so many people who knew me seemed to feel the need to tell the whole world about it.

This was additionally painful because I was already trying to repent of my errors. I was living a life devoted to Jesus Christ and the ministry of the gospel. I love Jesus and have given my life to sharing the good news of His gospel to the nations.

Still, many weren't convinced.

It would be long before the clamor over my sin would quiet down. It's one matter to have your most embarrassing secret displayed for the world to see; it's another entirely when that weak and wounded part of you is repeatedly criticized, constantly insulted, and oh-so-frequently slandered.

I just wanted to move on. I wanted to heal and walk with the Lord.

But so many people wouldn't let me.

GOSSIP IS A VICIOUS CYCLE. It creates a sense of "something's going on" that people have to talk about, or else they'll miss out on the big story. And since the story has to be riveting, gossipers are prone to exaggeration and overreaction. There's always a grain of truth to a piece of gossip, but it has undergone gross mutation by the time it reaches others' ears.

As word of my sins traveled literally around the world, I quickly learned who my true friends were. Having heard through the grapevine, my genuine friends reached out with care, seeking to minister, encourage, and restore me. However, seeing so many others choose to forsake me was deeply painful. For instance, one friend in Mexico whom I used to assist didn't even bother to give me a call. Instead, he sent me a hurtful text message, stating I should NEVER contact him or anyone from his ministry again.

Another friend from Africa was mysteriously angry at me when I called him. I was surprised when the line picked up, only for him to dismiss me with a malicious tone. Then the call abruptly ended.

I received bothersome emails. Two friends called me a liar for not telling them everything. Yet I acknowledged my sins and repented to everyone who asked about it. I have tried to be transparent with people, but some assume there must be more to the story, and to be my friend, they must know all the salacious details, which I beg to differ.

A beloved friend of mine abruptly ceased all communication, blocking my texts and phone calls. She went as far as unfriending me on social media. Then she made it clear to others that she wanted nothing to do with me. The pain of her rejection cut deeper than any physical wound; I would have preferred being stabbed with a knife to having been deleted like this.

Unfortunately, she was not the only one to distance herself from me. Another friend shared the heartbreaking news that we needed to sever our ties, driven by her husband's command to break all communication with me. Furthermore, a different friend removed me from social media and denied doing so, choosing to ignore my phone calls and texts.

Many others stopped talking to me too. I was treated as if I were a criminal who was wandering the streets. Even today, some individuals once held me in high regard but now want nothing to do with me. I bear a heaviness in my heart when I think about them, but it gives me an opportunity to pray for them and give this grief to the Lord rather than carrying it in my heart.

On the other hand, not everyone was so unforgiving. One dear friend arranged to meet with me and have an open-heart conversation. Despite feeling panged, he approached our meeting with patience and sympathy, reflecting a deep sense of consideration. He gently asked me questions and wholeheartedly listened to me.

In a separate instance, another friend had somehow been told about my sins. When he called, his tone carried genuine concern as he asked, "Is it true?" It was clear what he was referring to, and for the next thirty minutes, I answered his questions openly. Despite being hurt by my confession, he remained sincerely concerned for my well-being. After our conversation, we took the time to pray together on the phone, for which I am immensely grateful.

Over the months I received these communications, I also heard from acquaintances I had met during my travels for ministry around the United States. I was stunned to hear my struggles were being spread around without my consent. Apparently, "Pray for Lawrence" was nothing more than a vehicle to introduce the topic of my same-sex attraction into the conversation. Didn't these people realize they were using the name of Jesus to endorse their gossip?

Infuriated, I turned to prayer. I had to do something with this furious, gut-wrenching feeling other than lash out, as I had done in the past.

Still, more and more people reached out, asked, and reacted. What was I going to do?

After months of dealing with the humiliating phone calls, I was completely drained in every sense of the word. I had been betrayed a hundred times over. My name and reputation had been dragged through the mud in multiple countries. How was I supposed to cope with people's criticisms, negative comments, and judgment, all while losing friends by the day? I was shattered and hit a new low point in my life. I felt emotionally numb, and I even contemplated suicide.

Then God showed me a better way. I couldn't control what people thought of my sin; I couldn't change how they reacted to it and me.

Nevertheless, I could pray for them.

Every one of us struggles with sin. Some sins are spectacles to look at and talk about, like my transgressions; others are subtle and flow with the cultural current. Those who gossiped about me and judged me were giving into their own temptation. They needed prayer, as the only one who could save them from their sin was Jesus.

Just like me.

I began praying for my new *enemies*, those who were persecuting me.

But my anger didn't simply vanish. At times, it seemed to get somehow *worse*.

I began having vengeful thoughts. I wanted to call people back and curse them up and down for judging me. I wanted to travel over to people's homes, punch them in the face, and let them feel a smidgen of the pain I was feeling. Didn't they know how sinful *their* actions were? I didn't have to put up with it anymore, and there were times when I almost picked up the phone and started dialing.

Thankfully I had practice giving my anger to the Lord. I pleaded with God to help me let go of my bitterness and forgive those who had hurt me.

God heard my prayers!

One morning during my daily quiet time (devotions), I was reading a particular passage in the Bible that resonated with me deeply. As I read Psalm 141, verse 5, I knew God was giving me the answer on how to deal with slander. Psalm 141:5 says: "Let the righteous smite me; it shall be a kindness: and let him reprove me; it shall be an excellent oil, which shall not break my head: for yet my prayer also shall be in their calamities."

How should you and I deal with those who slander us and speak endlessly about our faults? What can we do if we've been a victim of slander?

The scripture offers invaluable wisdom on how to respond. It provides guidance on both internal and external responses, revealing a powerful strategy for dealing with those who have spread gossip about you. Moreover, it offers comfort and guidance.

The Bible says: "Let the righteous smite me; it shall be a kindness…" Christ, who put on human flesh and did not sin, allowed Himself to be smitten each and every day. He is our example, and we should follow His footsteps.

The "righteous" are all the people we hold dear: Christians, family members, friends, co-workers, etc. God instructs us to turn the other cheek and allow ourselves to be smitten. To "smite" means to strike, afflict or attack physically or mentally, causing sudden pain. When someone slanders us, they are smiting us, inflicting harm mentally and tangibly. In other words, God is cautioning if we find ourselves smeared, we should not be caught off guard; we should allow it to occur and endure its pain. We don't have to get ourselves all bent out of shape and retaliate; we can trust God.

But why would we choose to do this? Because "it shall be a kindness." In other words, God will turn their evil around to showcase His glory and extend favor to us. Amidst the pain, we have the potential to learn significant insights and develop godly compassion and temperament, which in turn can unlock forthcoming opportunities for God's grace, favor, and goodness. Kindness is a precious disposition that draws favor and blessings.

The verse continues: "...let him reprove me; it shall be an excellent oil, which shall not break my head..." God emphasizes that we can allow others to hold their disapproval of us. To "reprove" signifies criticism, strong disapproval, or censure. By enduring hardships with patience, God assures that all the tumult He holds in His hands will be transformed and utilized as "excellent oil." His oil is not like the temporary relief the world offers; instead, God's oil provides a lasting remedy that promotes healing, strength, and instruction toward an elevation of excellence.

If you are wondering if this approach is safe, God assures affirmatively, "[it] shall not break my head," as if to answer, "Yes." Your capacity to forgive the past, discern right from wrong, and lead others in the future will not be broken. Embracing and enduring slander is an opportunity for growth in character development, shaping us to demonstrate more gentleness, compassion, forgiveness, patience, and temperance. The result is our transformation into more adept leaders in ministry, at home, at work, and in the community.

The scripture concludes with a profound message: "…for yet my prayer also shall be in their calamities." It reminds us that God expects us to pray for those who have wronged us.

When we seek Him in *intercessory* prayer for our offenders, not solely for ourselves, the Lord will stand with us, granting us strength during our difficulties. Prayer does not so much change matters around us as it changes our hearts' disposition. As the Lord says in Romans 12:19, "Vengeance is mine; I will repay, saith the Lord." Thus, God will handle our offenders in His wise and timely manner. Therefore, our focus should be on aligning our hearts with God's perspective and praying for them, so that if judgment does come upon our offenders, we will not rejoice in their difficulties. Instead, we will serve them in their times of need with intercessory prayer.

It took me a considerable amount of time to grasp understanding and implement these valuable principles in my life. Embracing and applying them required immense humility, and by God's grace, my heart gradually softened. Nevertheless, the impact they've had on me has been tremendous. I've been blessed to dedicate countless hours to praying for those who spread the word about my sins abroad, earnestly seeking God's mercy on their behalf. As followers of Christ, our hearts should long for mercy over judgment and kindness over vengeance. Embracing this mindset opens us up to God's abundant blessings and favor throughout our lives.

I F WE BELIEVE THE GOSPEL, then our own perfection isn't the standard. *Christ's* perfection is. And that's all I can ever lay claim to.

It took a long time to forgive my brothers and sisters for how they judged me and put my life in a public space for ridicule. I spent days in agony, weeping and crying out for relief. Through much prayer, I embraced the humble spirit of Christ and learned to genuinely forgive those who wronged me.

A key to happiness that liberates us from the shackles of the past is forgiveness. It means letting go of past events and feelings of anger we mistakenly believe we must hold onto. Clinging onto negativity hinders our ability to find happiness. Forgiveness involves being open to seeing the offender in the light of love rather than fixating on the offense. It also consists in releasing the expectation that the past could have been different. Since we can't change the past, we should cast down all negative feelings associated with it and embrace the present. Forgiveness doesn't excuse wrongdoing inflicted upon you; instead, it acknowledges the wrong that occurred in your history. You decide to keep it in history and release the grip of the past, so now you can freely move forward with your life.

The factor that gave me the capacity to forgive and brought true peace was to remember how Jesus was rejected by His friends and beaten to death for a crime He didn't commit. And He forgave! He could sympathize with my sufferings and weaknesses. My God loves me that much, and He loves you that much too!

When others decide to judge us, we must run to the Just Judge in Heaven for our salvation. The Scriptures are abundantly clear that God's wrath—*all* of it—was poured out on Jesus on the cross. He was punished for all our sins, whether in the past, those in our hearts at this very moment, or even those you and I will commit before He shall takes us Home. He is faithful and just to wash us white as snow.

The judgment is satisfied because justice has been served. But the punishment wasn't laid on us; Jesus was condemned for our wrongdoings and crushed in our place.

This is no reason to go on sinning. As Paul writes in his letter to the Romans, "What shall we say then? Shall we continue in sin, that grace may abound? God forbid. How shall we, that are dead to sin, live any longer therein?" (Romans 6:1-2). I hate I'm still tempted to sin and there are moments when I succumb to its fatal influence!

But I am not a slave to sin or its threat to destroy me forever. Jesus has paid the price to take the power of sin away forever: "Christ hath redeemed us from the curse of the law, being made a curse for us..." (Galatians 3:13).

I will always have something for which to repent. So will everyone else until their day of judgment before the King of Kings.

But what gives me such hope and peace is God is a Just Judge, and the penalty has been met no matter what Satan tries to say. Even when he fools Christ's followers into thinking otherwise, the price of sin is paid in full. I am His son now, and Satan can do nothing to take that away.

Slander is brutal. The pain is unrelenting, like the crush of four concrete walls closing in around you.

But you don't have to bear it alone. Christ, too, was slandered and beaten by those who felt entitled to judge.

Praise be to God for the redemption of Jesus!

I know He will redeem me, too, for I am clothed in Christ's righteousness and not my own. I pray you find the same hope of His righteousness so when others slander you and curse you for your sins, you can repent in peace and trust God for your deliverance.

It isn't easy. It might be the most painful experience this life can offer.

But it is the ultimate test of one's faith.

Will you trust in Christ's righteousness to deliver you?

I pray more than ever that you do!

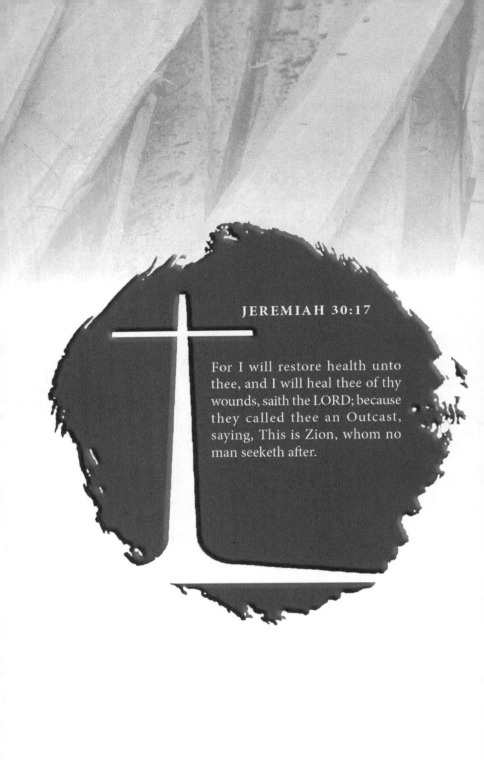

**JEREMIAH 30:17**

For I will restore health unto thee, and I will heal thee of thy wounds, saith the LORD; because they called thee an Outcast, saying, This is Zion, whom no man seeketh after.

## *Have You Considered*

# Why Do People Gossip and Spread Such Hurtful Words?

D O YOU EVER TALK about other people's sins? I've definitely been there. It can be a lot of fun to sit amongst friends and chat about others' indiscretions.

Yet Jesus warns us about this behavior. Jesus knows we are brilliant analysts of everyone else's sins but terrible students of our own.

"And why beholdest thou the mote that is in thy brother's eye, but considerest not the beam that is in thine own eye?" Jesus asked. "Or how wilt thou say to thy brother, Let me pull out the mote out of thine eye; and, behold, a beam is in thine own eye? Thou hypocrite, first cast out the beam out of thine own eye; and then shalt thou see clearly to cast out the mote out of thy brother's eye" (Matthew 7:3-5).

The metaphor compares specks of sawdust, or

"motes," to beams of wood. Clearly, one is larger and much more significant than the other. Jesus makes a bold statement when he declares we have beams in our own eyes, but we are too busy inspecting the eyes of others for wooden microbes.

Jesus' words are a dire warning for those of us who partake in gossip, slander, and discussions veiled as prayer requests concerning other people's sins. When we gossip about others, it proves we fail to recognize the beam within our own eyes. But if we trust His words, then we have to realize our sin is:

- Bigger than we think
- Worse than we think

When we gossip and slander, we cry to the masses about how awful the specks of sawdust are in the eyes of others. Yet Jesus makes it clear our own eyes are plagued with terrible, plank-sized infections.

"Your sin is bigger than you think," Jesus seems to say, "and worse than you think."

We are so prone to talk loudly about other people's specks of sawdust than our massive beam infections. This reveals how ignorant we are about our need for Jesus!

I wish my Christian brothers and sisters had considered Jesus' words before they slandered me to the world. Yet I also wish I had considered it when I judged them back, railed against them in my heart, and dragged my feet to forgive them.

We all need God's grace. We all need Jesus.

Judgment and condemnation are two of the devil's cruelest weapons, and he regularly uses them to cut and divide the Body of Christ. He sows mistrust, suspicion, and fear in our hearts, splitting us into rival factions.

This is precisely what Jesus wanted us *not* to do. Prior to His arrest and crucifixion, Jesus prayed, "Neither pray I for these alone, but for them also which shall believe on me through their word; *That they all may be one; as thou, Father, art in me, and I in thee, that they also may be one in us:* that the world may believe that thou hast sent me. And the glory which thou gavest me I have given them; that they may be one, even as we are one: I in them, and thou in me, that they may be made perfect in one; and that the world may know that thou hast sent me, and hast loved them, as thou hast loved me" (John 17:20-23, emphasis added).

Just as the Father, Jesus, and the Holy Ghost are one, we, God's children, must be united. We are not to let fear and judgment divide us. Jesus clearly commands us to love and be reconciled to one another.

Yet gossip and slander set us at odds, making our hearts cold and bitter.

We must turn aside our fears. We must set aside our trivial differences. God's love and grace are timeless, offering us hope for peace in this world and the next.

I pray no matter what you've done or who you are, you receive God's grace with open arms and believe He loves you and is eager to sanctify you.

Don't let Satan's weapon cut you away from fellowship with Jesus. Don't let the judgment of others, or your impulse to judge, be the false gospel you believe.

Trust in Christ, and trust in the power of the cross.

**LUKE 9:23**

And he said to them all, If any man will come after me, let him deny himself, and take up his cross daily, and follow me.

*Ten*

# OBEDIENCE
## When God Demands Everything

THE TURN OF THE CENTURY, I was living the American Dream before God tricked me into ministry and sent me to Africa, Asia, and all across Latin America. My business was booming, meaning I could live a wondrous lifestyle for all to envy in one of the most expensive real estate markets in the United States. I owned a beautiful San Diego home and did whatever I pleased. My wanderlust took me across the world on wonderful vacations, eager to explore and see everything I acquired to make myself happy and content. My kitchen boasted exquisite dinner plates, my drinkware was crafted from crystal, and my silverware was composed of pure silver from Tiffany's. Everything was going unimaginably well.

Then God told me to give it all up.

When I graduated college, I set my sights on California. I wanted to get as far away from boring Ohio as possible. I wanted to live somewhere beautiful, in a city where wealthy, extravagant, and successful people thrive. I wanted to be independent and prove myself to the world.

In a matter of months, I decided to set God and the Christian life aside. After years participation in college ministry, I had come to a sticking point: Why had God allowed such terrible incidents to happen to me, only for me to *serve Him* in return? In my mind, it wasn't fair, and I was going to explore other options for my provision. I wanted to experience all the glittery attractions of the world. And that's all I would find out the world can offer.

I didn't abandon my faith completely; I couldn't, as the Spirit was still living in me and calling out to the Father on my behalf. Oddly enough, I still felt a sense of fear toward God, and therefore, I committed to continue reading a chapter of the Bible each day, but I would have nothing to do with any church, nor did I want to associate with Christians. From my point of view, God had let me down. He owed me a season of freedom.

For the next three years, I chased whatever my flesh desired, accumulating many signs of worldly success. A comfortable home. A new car. Exquisite furniture and beautiful décor. Stylish clothing, shoes, and fashionable rings. And, of course, the address in San Diego. To my loved ones, I was a wild success, and they all congratulated me on the good I was doing.

................
200

As the years passed by, I only grew more and more miserable inside. During the initial two years, the frequent visits to dance clubs, the dining at delicious restaurants, associations with affluent peers, and the ceaseless acquisition of worldly possessions seemed to transport me to paradise. But it rapidly faded and left me feeling aimless and inadequate. Loneliness crept to the point my sumptuous home felt more like a prison. My license to go wherever I pleased became a reminder I had no reason to go on other than my selfish desires.

Still, I read my daily chapter of the Bible more out of a sense of duty than genuine devotion, as if to prove a point to God I could somehow be hedonistic and holy at the same time. Over and over, His Word reminded me He desired fellowship with me. He beckoned me to rely on Him for my provision rather than leaning on a business and godless friends. God longed for the opportunity to be my love and passion, not solely to supply physical goods that rust and moth destroy and thieves break in and steal. He convicted me of sin and reminded me of how selfish and empty sin is.

Before I knew it, I found myself openly muttering to myself about how much I missed fellowshipping with other believers and discussing the greatness of God in our lives. I missed the palpable presence of Jesus, not because He wasn't available, but because I had shut Him out of my life. Most of all, I missed the beauty of living in service of the Almighty God, trusting in Him completely, and walking in His ways.

Finally, I set out to find a church. I skimmed through

the internet to find local churches. Each Sunday, I would get up early and drive to a new place and check it out. My search was incredibly discouraging. I couldn't believe how many churches resembled dance clubs. The dimmed lights, worldly styles of music, and other gimmicks felt like a farce to me. I was trying to distance myself from that scene, but all I could find were churches offering a similar experience under the guise of worshiping God.

After several months of praying and searching, I found one that avoided many worldly, seeker-friendly tropes that failed to truly engage in worship and learning of Jesus Christ the Lord. The preaching was spot-on, strongly emphasizing the Bible, and the teaching and preaching were insightful and convicting. The singing was Christ-honoring and simply beautiful. Most importantly, people referred to the Lord by His name, Jesus Christ, recognizing the power of His name rather than simply as *God*.

I began attending regularly, not only on Sunday mornings but Sunday evenings and midweek services. Throughout the following year, my understanding of God's grace grew tremendously, and my faith replenished much of what I had lost in my season of selfish materialism. My courage and zeal for the gospel swelled, and I began to share the Good News of Jesus with many people I met throughout my days.

Thankfully, I was no longer pretending I didn't need a Saviour. But I was still enjoying many of the fruits of my American Dream. I felt a constant, nagging sense I wasn't really asking God to be Lord over my life. Culturally, Americans are very averse to the idea of a lord or king. Nevertheless Jesus is quite plain when He declares, "Before Abraham was, I am," meaning He is Lord of all things, including time itself (John 8:58). Jesus didn't come to earth to die and rise from the dead merely to be my friend or helper (though He certainly is those things!). He conquered sin, death, and guilt so I can finally have a Good and True King. After chasing all the false ideals of this world and returning empty, I was hungry to depend on a King who promised never to let me down.

But to do that, I would have to trust Him completely. And so I began to seek the Lord and pray often, asking Him how I would do that.

That's when the Spirit spoke clearly within my heart: "Close your business."

I refused. How was I supposed to shutter my business and continue to pay the bills? Didn't God understand simple economics?

I tried to bargain with the Almighty.

"I'll tithe more!" I promised. "Whatever it takes to please You, Lord: 15%, 20% of everything I make. I'll volunteer in more church ministries. Just don't take my business from me, God!"

But the message was clear and unwavering. Over the next several months, the Spirit moved in my heart, and every Scriptural passage I read had the same theme that is best summarized by the well-known proverb of Solomon: "Trust in the Lord with all thine heart; and lean not unto thine own understanding. In all thy ways acknowledge him, and he shall direct thy paths" (Proverbs 3:5-6).

Pursuing my business endeavors seemed entirely logical from my perspective and comprehension. However, deciding to close it and yielding to God's will compelled me to place my complete trust in the Lord and rely on Him to guide my journey.

It was simple yet oh-so-difficult.

For months I refused to act. Looking back, I'm incredibly grateful for God's patience. What a wonderful Father He is to lead us and tenderly wait on us to trust His ways! Through additional Scripture reading, the Lord highlighted the abundance of His wealth. God reminded me He owns everything, including the rolling hills and the cattle which graze on them. God vividly pointed out He didn't require or want my money. What difference would an additional 5, 10, or 50% make to His vast storehouses? God wanted something much rarer and more precious: my heart!

God had me cornered. I knew God was asking me to do something surpassing my capabilities, and I realized I needed to obey. However, I became increasingly stubborn. I attempted to brainstorm alternative solutions, but my efforts were futile, and I couldn't find a way out of my predicament. A year had elapsed since I first prayed and committed to whatever God asked of me. However, I still resisted the one task He had pressed upon my heart to do.

The day finally came when God must have decided

the time for patience had ended and the time for action had arrived. One morning, while sitting at my dining room table reading my Bible, I read my daily passage and did not think of anything else. No one was in my home except for me; the only sounds were those of the birds outside.

Suddenly, without warning, I heard the sound of a man's voice directly in front of me. It spoke boldly and asked the most profound question: "If you die today, do you want to be remembered as a successful businessman or someone who loved Jesus?"

The voice was as clear and piercing as light, and I knew God was speaking to me. Without hesitation, I blurted out, "Someone who loves Jesus."

Then the voice spoke again: "Then shut down your business."

The moment I heard those words, I felt something touch me within my chest, right on my heart. It was as if God was pressing on my heart with His finger: God's call to action. Perhaps, I thought with much inner turmoil, it was His final ultimatum, as a parent making a last demand. The thought filled me with fear because I knew when God becomes silent about something, it's a dangerous place to be. Although I was terrified to shut down my business, a whisper of courageous faith began to stir within me. I decided right then to believe God and follow through with His leadings.

During the following months, I initiated the process of closing down the business.

I had no idea how I would pay my bills. I had no idea

what else I would do for income. These questions had yet to be answered.

And it would be some time before answers would come. For a time, I would be tested beyond any of my existing limits. Metal must be purified by fire before it gains true strength.

So it would be for me, especially when the bank foreclosed on my home and I was forced to walk away into the dark of night with nowhere to go.

1 PETER 2:21-23

For even hereunto were ye called: because Christ also suffered for us, leaving us an example, that ye should follow his steps:

## *Have You Considered*

# Embracing God's Purpose When You Are Suffering?

SUFFERING IS AN INEVITABLE PART of our lives. It can come in many forms, such as physical or mental pain, emotional distress, or challenging circumstances. When we experience suffering, it's natural to feel discouraged, helpless, and alone. However, we Christians have a unique perspective on enduring difficult times.

At the heart of our faith, we find the assurance that suffering, as paradoxical as it may seem, is a puzzle piece that, though painful and perplexing at times, ultimately fits snugly into the grand design of our life's beautiful journey. The Bible instructs us to rejoice even in the midst of suffering (Romans 5:3-5 and James 1:2-4). There is a purpose behind it. We are not alone in our afflictions. We have God, who is the very essence of life. Additionally, there are people worldwide who experience much more severe pain than we do. We can take comfort in the fact we are not alone and we share the common human experience with others.

Suffering can serve as an opportunity for us to grow closer to God. Have you ever prayed for God to use you or to help you draw nearer to Him? Even if those prayers were made years ago and have slipped from memory, God has not forgotten them. When we experience suffering, it could very well be God's response to those prayers. It may not be in the way we anticipated or desired, but we can trust His ways are higher than ours, and everything happens according to His will is ultimately a blessing, even if it may not feel pleasant at the moment. Even if we did not expect or desire the suffering, we can rest assured God uses it for our good and His glory.

If you doubt whether you can handle the sufferings that come your way, your doubts are correct; you won't be able to endure the afflictions on your own. But God can and will handle them for you.

It's essential to remember suffering is ultimately for Christ's sake. Embracing His will amid difficulties is vital. Despite the challenge of finding joy in despair, we're called to rejoice in weakness. By doing so, we shift from self-reliance and pride to turning toward God. We develop confidence in God's ability as we yield to let Him bear our burdens, recognizing our insufficiency to carry them.

So how do we find joy in our suffering for the sake of Christ? It is through God's grace; His grace is more than enough for us. We can humbly seek God for additional grace to empower us to fulfill His will in our lives and those around us. Consider the words of 2 Corinthians 12:10, which beautifully state, "I take pleasure in infirmities, in reproaches, in necessities, in persecutions, in distresses for Christ's sake..." These are the very trials the Lord permits for His glory, and it is not our strength that sustains us but the strength He imparts within us.

Suffering serves as a humble reminder of our dependence in God. In moments of weakness, we find strength through Christ, who gives us the power to endure and persevere. We can take comfort in knowing our suffering is not meaningless but holds a significant purpose within God's plan. Even hardships can lead us to a deeper understanding of God, a profound truth beautifully exemplified in the life of Job.

Job was an intelligent, prominent man who feared God and lived a righteous life. However, he endured immense suffering and loss. Amid his afflictions, he learned a valuable lesson: God is the LORD, seated on the throne, while Job was merely a humble servant. And, Job willingly submitted, trusting God's sovereignty without argument (Job 42:1-6). Through this challenging journey, Job gained a deeper understanding of God's character, and eventually was restored to a place of abundance and blessing. The principal concern of God's plan for our lives is that we recognize and submit to His lordship, holiness, and the reverence and honor due to Him.

Undoubtedly, suffering is an excellent tool to help us learn these truths.

If you are going through challenging times, always remember you are not alone. While it's natural to seek relief and ask God to alleviate the pain, it's equally essential to yield to His will and allow Him to provide the strength to endure. You can take comfort in the knowledge God accompanies you through every step of the journey, and His grace is more than enough to sustain you.

God's allowance of suffering has been a question asked by countless people for many years. However, the Bible illustrates a thorn in the flesh that sheds some light on this topic. This thorn is like having a large tack or needle stuck in our skin, which cannot be readily removed. It's not a tiny thorn which can easily be plucked away. Worse, when we try to remove it ourselves, part of it breaks off and remains lodged within us indefinitely, causing intermittent pain. This pain may persist because it's meant to be there, and we're meant to learn from it. It's *supposed* to hurt. There are particular thorns in the flesh God gives us to stay with us and periodically cause us pain *necessary* for our spiritual growth.

The Apostle Paul found himself with a thorn in the flesh. He prayed to God three times to have it removed, but it was not granted. God had a reason for allowing the thorn to remain, as it served a greater purpose in Paul's life and was ultimately for his benefit. Similarly, the suffering or pain we experience may be a blessing in disguise, even though it doesn't seem like it because it hurts. It might stick with us for a long time, but it's meant to transform us into the image of Christ, humble us, and help us develop the necessary characteristics to be useful in God's plan.

God enables us to suffer because He loves us. God assures us it is for our good. It may even remain with us for the rest of our lives because it serves a divine purpose. By enduring pain, we become more yielding, which in turn allows us to be more influentially used by God.

It's crucial to understand suffering is not a punishment from God but a part of His plan for us. He can use it to bring about good and to honor Christ. While we may not always understand why we must go through the hardship, we can trust God has a purpose for our pain.

We must bear in mind there are occasions when, despite our heartfelt pleas, God's response might be a resolute "no." He knows the reasons behind our suffering and will employ it for our ultimate benefit. Consequently, we must maintain our trust in Him and permit His work within us as we navigate through trials. Each of us encounters distinct challenges permitted by God as a component of His unique plan for us. The nature of our afflictions may vary from person to person, but we can place our faith in the assurance God has a purpose explicitly tailored for each one of them.

Embracing pain can be a challenging yet necessary part of our growth and transformation to become like Christ. He endured suffering; we too, will encounter moments of pain. In the midst of these trials, we can draw comfort from the knowledge that God's boundless grace is sufficient to carry us through each difficult moment.

As Christians, we have a lively hope that transcends

this world (1 Peter 1:3). The suffering we endure is but only a temporary passing phase, and we eagerly anticipate the day when all pain and sorrow will be banished. In eternity, alongside God and our fellow brethren in Christ, we shall be immersed in never-ending joy and peace, liberated from all burdens and trials.

Therefore, we should not wallow in self-pity or let our suffering define us. There will be no moment like this again. Rather, we should find a way to let Jesus be in it. Find a cause for rejoicing in Christ amidst trials, knowing God will use our afflictions to mold us into the individuals He wants us to become. Placing our trust in Him, we can rest assured He will bring forth goodness from our pain, both for our benefit and to glorify Christ's name.

**PSALM 55:22**

Cast thy burden upon the LORD, and he shall sustain thee: he shall never suffer the righteous to be moved.

*Eleven*

# D O U B T
# Things Fall Apart

HOW DOES ONE ACQUIRE FAITH? Is it learned? Received? Built through a long process?

The answer is probably a bit of 'Yes' to all three. It certainly was for me.

Looking back, I'm grateful I had no idea what would happen to me after closing my business, or else I would not have done it. No amount of trust or faith would have led me down that path. Only by following God one step at a time and trusting Him could I take such perilous steps.

In those early San Diego years, my faith was weak. I had only recently begun getting involved in a couple of ministries at my church, prison and street evangelism ministries. But I had never experienced God doing anything so significant before this. While I remembered how gracious and helpful God had been in guiding me to college, paying my bills, and leading me to San Diego, on the other hand, shutting down a profitable business was something I couldn't fathom.

The response from my loved ones wasn't helpful, either. To them, my situation seemed ideal and I was doing exceptionally well. The American Dream was safe and secure in my hand, so why would I ever give it up? They questioned my judgment and spiritual insight; some even dared to say I had *not* heard from God. They urged me to double down on my bargain, to tithe two or three times my normal portion.

Looking back, I don't fault these loved ones for thinking this way. Our culture is an ocean of influence and persuasion, and when we live in it all our lives, we can't help but want to swim with the current. However, Jesus was anything but complacent with the culture; He railed against its momentum and modeled radical dependence on His Heavenly Father. When God calls to us, He rarely asks us to do something within the cultural norm. In the world, it is commendable to build your own business and depend on your strong work ethic. In the Kingdom of Heaven, it is commendable to depend on God's work ethic and ask Him, "What will You have me do for the glory and honor of Jesus Christ?"

Yet even in closing my business, I retained a sense of self-assurance and a touch of conceit. I assumed securing a new job would be a breeze. After all, I was fluent in Spanish, a college graduate, well-traveled with a wealth of cultural understanding, and blessed with a network of connections garnered through my successful entrepreneurship in the region.

Little did I know God would strip all this away, removing all avenues. "For thou shalt worship no other god," Moses wrote in Exodus, "for the LORD, whose name is Jealous, is a jealous God" (Exodus 34:14). In English, the word "jealous" carries a connotation of petty or envious. But here, we must see God strictly for who He is: the One and Only True God. All others are false, imaginary beings, empowered merely by Satan and his lesser minions. God is a jealous God; His jealousy is akin to how a bride or bridegroom should crave the exclusive love of a spouse. God has no interest in sharing my dependence with another that cannot indeed provide.

To help me recognize the extent of my need for Him, God would have to take drastic measures. I had built quite the secular profile and had plenty of skills, assets, and connections on which I could boast. I had bootstraps, so to speak, and I was ready to pull myself up if circumstances got rough.

Once I closed my business, I created multiple resumes and embarked on a job search. Initially, I reached out to business acquaintances and aimed for executive and higher administrative positions, but my endeavors ended in disappointment. Undeterred, I shifted my focus to management positions across various industries, only to encounter similar setbacks. I expanded my search to include jobs in multiple categories, and over the course of a year, I filled out hundreds of applications, spoke with countless people, and applied for over 1,000 jobs. My relentless efforts produced nothing; only a handful of companies even granted me the chance to interview. Surprisingly, even entry-level positions at fast food joints or major retailers would not give me a job.

What was going on? I had worked hard to make a big deal of myself in the San Diego professional market. How was it that no one—*literally no one*—considered me a valuable addition to their team?

I was crushed.

To compound matters, some of my friends made hurtful comments at my expense. One friend, trying to be helpful, put his arm around me and said, "You know, Lawrence, the Bible says if you don't work, you shouldn't eat." Although I felt like snapping back at him with rebuke, the Holy Spirit urged my spirit to remain silent. I stood there in complete grief, saying nothing in response.

Instead, I prayed to God, pleading with Him to provide a job. Despite my persistent search efforts and active approach, all opportunities seemed to elude me.

As my savings dwindled, I found myself with no alternative but to sell off my belongings. It was especially difficult to part with my cherished collection of crystal vases from Tiffany. This process persisted until I had emptied my life of everything material. With no other recourse, I had to turn to food stamps and government assistance, a profoundly humbling journey, to say the least. Within months, my reality had shifted drastically—from savoring meals at Southern California's finest restaurants to sitting in a dingy government office, surrounded by individuals I once judged for their perceived imprudent and sinful choices.

Before long, I was many months late on my mortgage payments, and the bank was demanding repayment. I had nothing left to offer them. The bank went to the courts, and after many more months, the bank finally proceeded with foreclosing on my home. Reluctantly, I was forced to hand over my keys to the bank's realtor, acknowledging the inevitable. I signed the necessary paperwork, and I left with nothing but the clothes on my back and car.

Walking away from my foreclosed home, I felt nothing but gut-wrenching despair. Had God set me up to fail? I had trusted Him and obeyed His command. What, then, was this insanity?

Overwhelmed by uncertainty, I was left feeling numb and utterly helpless, contemplating my next steps and where I should go. My pride held me back from seeking help or confiding in anyone. Aimlessly, I drove through the streets without any clear direction for the night. Eventually, I found myself on a road dotted with real estate signs. The Great Recession hit this avenue hard, as numerous houses had been foreclosed on and abandoned. I slowed the car, heaved a deep sigh that felt like I hadn't breathed in a year, and then parked on the dark street.

Thanks to my business connections, I had access to the San Diego MLS website, where I could browse the current real estate listings on the market and retrieve the lockbox codes. Seated in my car, I diligently searched for the combination to unlock the front door. Once I found it, I sat in my car for a few minutes to gather my thoughts. At last, I mustered the courage to step out of the vehicle, locking the door behind me.

With a pillow and blanket in hand, I trudged up the silent concrete path, taking slow, cautious steps toward the dark, uninhabited house. Creeping to the porch, I looked through the windows and pressed my ear against the door. I waited for an eternity, listening for any sound of squatters or meth addicts lurking inside. After a reassuring silence, I unlocked the combination box housing the key. Then I unlocked the door and quietly slipped inside.

The interior was carpeted, dry, and layered with a smidgen of dust. A small pile of garbage lay on the kitchen floor, but most of the house was clean. It appeared in need of a family. It was eerie, empty, and silent. Tonight, it was all mine.

I walked back to the dining room. It had the thickest carpet. I threw my pillow on the floor near a wall and crawled down onto the floor. I laid my head on the pillow and covered myself with my blanket.

Was I really about to sleep in an abandoned house? Was this indeed where God had led me?

I closed my eyes.

I could get it all back. Just reinstate the business, make a few phone calls to old connections, and get the money train chugging once again. It wouldn't be too hard. All it would take is some sweat and swallowed pride. Admit you were an idiot, Lawrence. You misunderstood what God was telling you. Maybe He wanted 25% of your income. That was all He wanted, and you missed it.

"Why did You do this to me, God?" I moaned. "Why, why?"

I lay there feeling like a complete failure and cried, repeatedly asking God that same question until I finally drifted into a restless version of sleep.

FOR THE NEXT COUPLE OF MONTHS, I stayed at a friend's house while he was working in another city. However, his landlord discovered I was staying there without permission and promptly demanded I vacate the premises. Despite my assurances that I was a clean, professional person simply going through a difficult time, the landlord refused and threatened to evict my friend if I didn't leave.

After storing my belongings elsewhere, I found myself without a place to call home again. I had been keeping my financial struggles a secret from those around me, and even when I stayed with friends for a few nights, I tried to downplay the severity of my situation. However, they eventually figured out I was homeless, and their expressions revealed a mixed gaze of concern and trepidation. Although they were willing to help, I could tell they were anxious about the possibility of me overstaying my welcome. I expressed my gratitude for their kindness and moved on to another friend's home to spare them further discomfort. Unfortunately, the same pattern repeated itself with my other friends.

Initially, I felt frustrated and let down by my friends, as

I sensed a lack of loyalty when I needed them most. However, rather than succumbing to anger and disappointment, I turned to God, kneeling in prayer for my friends. Surprisingly, God filled my heart with compassion and empathy. I realized they, too, had their struggles and limitations, and it was unfair to expect unwavering support from friends. If God could show me love and mercy, I had the duty to extend the same to others, including my friends. Grateful for my friends' few days of assistance, I moved on with no ill feelings toward them.

Still, I had run out of options. I had run out of friends' homes to crash each night. With nowhere else to turn, I pleaded with God for assistance, weeping uncontrollably in my car. Despite my desperate cries, it felt as though no one on this earth could hear me and an overwhelming sense of loneliness and despair consumed me. My worst fear had come true. I was frozen in place, unable to think or act, and could only cry and agonize in my car, with no one to turn to for help.

Suddenly, an idea struck me: I could call David and Sandy Perry, my trusted mentors from Ohio. Maybe they could offer some helpful advice or even extend a helping hand. It was worth a shot.

I dialed David and Sandy's number from my cell phone with trembling hands. The clock had long since passed midnight in Ohio, and surprisingly Sandy answered the phone, groggy and disoriented. Tears streaming down my face, I struggled to explain my dire situation through sobs and gasps. "Sandy," I managed to choke out, "I'm...I'm homeless."

The weight of my words hung heavily in the air as

my friend processed the news on the other end of the line.

"Lawrence," she said, her voice tender, "that's terrible. Where are you?"

I explained I was in my car with nowhere to go.

"I'm so sorry this is happening to you," she said. "I wish I knew someone else in that area, but all I have is you, my friend."

"Please," I said, "anything you can offer me."

My friend thought for a moment, the silence thick between us. "Well, we are so far apart that I can't do anything for you right now. But I can offer you this. Do you remember what Jesus said about following Him in the Gospel of Matthew?"

I shook my head. I couldn't remember much of anything at that moment. "No," I whimpered.

"'Foxes have holes, and the birds of the air have nests; but the Son of man hath not where to lay his head,'" she recited (Matthew 8:20).

"Okay," I said, unsure what she was getting at.

"Jesus was homeless, too, Lawrence," Sandy said. "He had nowhere to lay His head. Think about it: Jesus asked others to follow Him throughout His ministry. Some didn't realize the cost and desired to follow Him while still desiring to hold on to their previous lives."

I nodded. It was beginning to make sense.

But it still didn't solve my problem of having nowhere to go that night. "Thank you, Sandy," I said. "I appreciate your encouragement."

"I know this must be very difficult for you, but I trust

you'll get through it," she said. "Don't forget Jesus knows how this feels; only He can relate to what you're experiencing. You're going to get through this, Lawrence."

I sniffed and wiped my nose. "Thank you, Sandy," I said.

As we ended the call, a lightness filled me, a sensation I hadn't felt since I signed the foreclosure papers. Jesus *did* know what this was like.

But how would that help me find a place to sleep that night?

Unfortunately, I had to go house-hunting once again, sneaking in and listening for the sounds of tweaking drug addicts who might mug me for whatever cash I had to buy another score. I avoided the worst, found another soft floor to make for my bed, and tried again to sleep in a borrowed house.

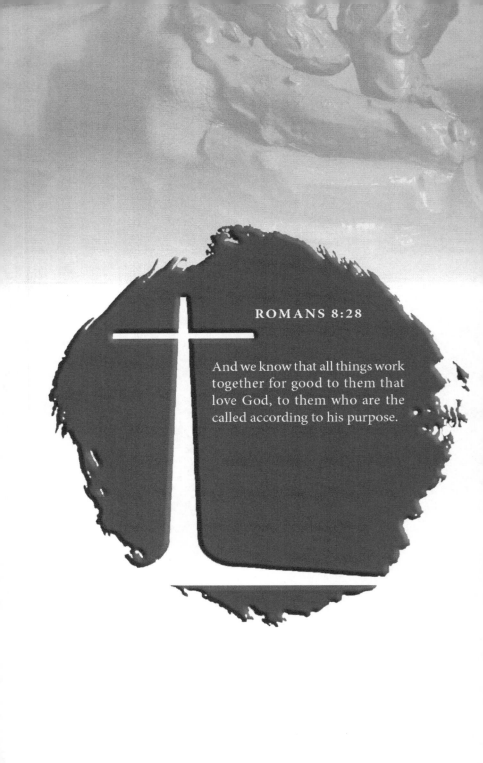

**ROMANS 8:28**

And we know that all things work together for good to them that love God, to them who are the called according to his purpose.

*Have You Considered*

# What the Devil Means for Evil, God Can Turn for Good?

WHEN I WAS FORCED to sleep in an abandoned house, I figured God had left me for good. After all, how could He be loving and loyal while I was in such a predicament?

This is one of the problems with equating God's goodness to societal success. It's easy to look at a wealthy person and assume they are "blessed" because of their physical comforts versus a homeless beggar who seems to be "cursed" or neglected by the Father. Yet the spiritual world is unlike the world we see and hear daily. In fact, I have found God is in the business of taking what Satan means for evil and upending it for His glory in the most surprising ways.

We'll come to the conclusion of my homelessness story shortly, but for a moment, I would like to reveal the miracle of God's grace in my life in a different area: my same-sex attraction. Through my abuse, Satan twisted aspects of my perspective in an attempt to corrupt me and turn me away from God. Yet by devoting myself to the gospel and trusting in the Lord more than my desires, I've been able to minister to people in ways few others have the opportunity to do.

I must mention it wasn't my choice for others to know this was a struggle. As I wrote before, the slander of others put my most intimate struggles into the public light for so many to see. However, God has used even this to bring about redemption and beauty, as He is so often able to do when we cry out to Him.

Numerous individuals have contacted me in strict confidence, seeking a safe environment to discuss this taboo topic. Their hearts are burdened with fear of judgment and long for understanding and discretion. They are also anxious to find reassurance God's love is steadfast and that they can continue to follow Jesus through the struggles.

Among those who have approached me are many men seeking prayer in utmost confidentiality. They feel like an outcast, unsure of what to do, confiding in me because they believe I am the only one who understands. I provide a safe space for them to open their hearts and share their anxious thoughts, where afterward we always conclude by praying for each other.

On one occasion, I received a heartfelt call from a dear wife who wanted to confide in me about her husband. They had fallen in love years ago, built a beautiful life together, and raised several children. However, recently, she discovered her husband had been struggling with same-sex attraction for a long time, keeping it hidden. He loved her but had broken his marriage vows and engaged in a secret affair with one of his buddies. I must emphasize I do not condone his adultery. He had made a solemn covenant with her and God to remain faithful solely to her.

This poor woman needed help from someone who would respect her privacy and handle her painful situation delicately. She sought guidance from someone who has experienced struggles firsthand and understood the challenges. Above all, she desired understanding from God's Word about her bewilderment, knowing the Bible alone could lead them towards healing and reconciliation.

She is one of the many individuals who have reached out to me. These troubles, I have come to realize, are quite common and affect families from all walks of life. Unfortunately, many individuals live in fear and desperately want help, even respected servants of God. For instance, in my ministry travels, I have served alongside exceptional missionaries, and occasionally I've encountered respectable families who have confided in me about a loved one struggling with same-sex attraction, keeping it guarded as a family secret.

In a particular encounter with a missionary family, I sensed in my spirit something was burdening their hearts. They had worked diligently over the years to reach their foreign community for Christ and make a lasting impact.

Nonetheless, I keenly discerned they were grappling with the complexities of a spirit of homosexuality. Despite recognizing this, I kept my thoughts to myself and silently prayed. Then, as we gathered around the dinner table, they nervously opened up, "Lawrence, we need to talk to you."

A sense of relief overcame me that they had the courage to open up. That evening, this beloved couple poured their hearts out to me. They revealed one of their children had recently moved to the United States and had become involved in the gay community. Learning their son was living with his boyfriend devastated them. They struggled to comprehend how their son, who was raised doing the Lord's work, had deviated from his faith to embrace a gay lifestyle. During our heartfelt conversation, I tried to offer some comfort and insight, knowing my words could only offer so much solace. Privately, I continue to pray for them and their family, hoping for healing and understanding in their journey.

I have to confess there have been times when I too have succumbed to temptation. Allowing myself to be in the wrong place for too long often has led to my downfall. I have come to recognize just like any heterosexual, I must be vigilant daily about what my eyes see, what my ears hear, what my nose smells, and where I am. I have to be conscious of my surroundings. If I don't, a slight distraction here and another distraction there will work together to lure me into temptation and potentially sin. My past experiences have taught me I must swiftly flee temptation and remove myself from such situations. Like anyone else, regardless of attractions, Satan uses countless tactics to deceive us into prioritizing our desires over God's design. Therefore, I must be resolute in trusting God's design and not be swayed by these enticements.

Still, I'm thankful God has transformed my naysayers' sinister actions into an exceptional ministry opportunity. Everyone who struggles with sin needs to be heard and helped. This is why Jesus referred to the Holy Spirit as the "Comforter"—we need His divine help and encouragement to make it through the gauntlet of life. I have been blessed to comfort others who struggle with same-sex attraction or are close to someone who does. There is no sin so terrible it excludes a sinner from the blood of Jesus and the gift of repentance and reconciliation, except for blasphemy (denying the Spirit's call to Christ). All sinners have access to God's forgiveness and redemption.

Satan does all he can to throw us into doubt and despair. God takes the broken pieces and makes them whole again, often more beautiful than before.

If He can do that for someone like me, then I know He absolutely can do just that for you, too.

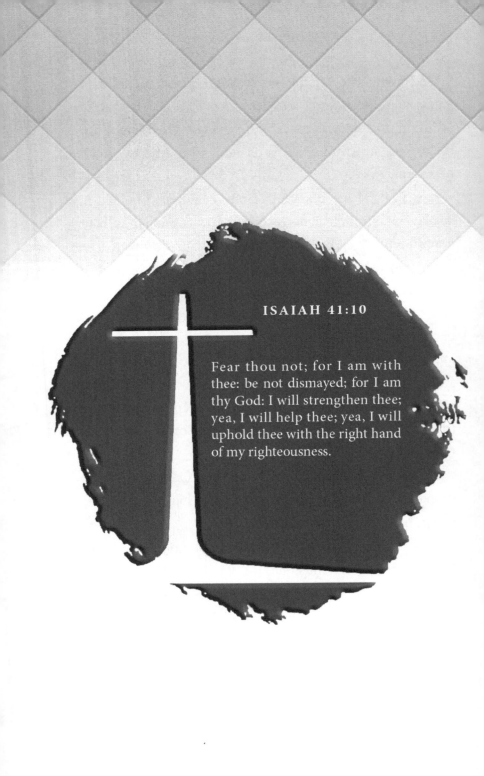

**ISAIAH 41:10**

Fear thou not; for I am with thee: be not dismayed; for I am thy God: I will strengthen thee; yea, I will help thee; yea, I will uphold thee with the right hand of my righteousness.

## Twelve

---

# HUMILIATION
## A New Wolf Appears

BEING HOMELESS SHOWED ME things I never thought I'd see.

When I first stood in line to get food stamps, they were a source of shame. Now they were literal life and death. With provisions in hand, I could eat enough to sustain myself while I waited for God to reveal the next step. I managed to maintain a basic membership at a local gym which charged me an incredible price of only $50 a year, enabling me to take daily showers and maintain my hygiene. This became my routine for the foreseeable future.

As night approached each day, I would grow increasingly anxious about where I would sleep. Would I have to resort to sleeping in more abandoned homes, risking violence and murder at the hands of hoodlums? Or would I find myself uncomfortably wedged in the back seats of my car or some other uncomfortable location to sleep?

I kept racking my brain for alternatives. Finally, an idea suddenly struck me—I could reach out to someone in San Diego on social media for assistance. Though my laptop's battery life was limited, I remembered a library in the city with electrical outlets conveniently located outside one of the side entrances. I made my way there and plugged in my laptop, accessing the free internet. Seated on the sidewalk late at night, I joined an AOL San Diego chat room, fervently praying for divine intervention and hoping someone would be willing to help me out.

With trembling fingers, I typed out my plea in the San Diego chat room: "I need help, please. I'm newly homeless and desperately need a safe place to sleep tonight. If anyone could offer me a place to stay, even for just one night, I would be incredibly grateful. Thank you." I hit "send" and waited, my heart racing with anticipation and hope.

I stared at the screen, my hope fading as the minutes passed without a response. I decided to try again, copying and pasting my plea multiple times into the thread. Despite my efforts, no one responded to my distress. Instead, a few people replied with unkind comments, telling me to "shut up" or "get a hotel room." I felt defeated and hopeless. Why were people so resistant to helping those in need?

After what felt like an eternity, a private message finally appeared on my screen. It was from a man who explained he owned a mattress store in the North Park area.

He told me he had lived in the back of his store since his wife passed away six months ago. We chatted briefly, and he kindly offered me a place to stay for the night. It wasn't exactly what I had hoped for, but it was a safe and warm place to rest my head. For that, I was genuinely thankful.

I made my way back to my car and drove to the store. As I arrived, I found it precisely where he had indicated in the chat. Simultaneously curious but anxious, I parked my car and approached the front doors, walking through the dark and eerily empty parking lot.

I knocked on the glass doors, and almost instantly, a heavyset man around 60 years old gently opened the lock and greeted me with a warm smile.

"Are you Lawrence?" he asked.

"Yes," I said, nodding. "Thank you so much."

"Do you have any drugs or weapons on you?"

"No, sir," I said. I patted the backpack that was slung over my shoulder and smiled. "Just my laptop."

"Come in," he said, waving me through the door. "Welcome to my mattress store. It's not much, but it's what my wife and I built together."

I stepped inside the store. Like most mattress stores, it had queen beds strewn about with colorful placards beside each, noting the brand and price. The man's welcoming demeanor immediately put me at ease as we strolled through the store and chatted. Towards the back of the establishment, he led me to his private living quarters. These comprised of a small living room, bedroom, office, and a tiny kitchen.

We settled into his cozy living room, illuminated by the soft glow of two lamps.

As I sat, I couldn't help but notice the multitude of pictures of his beloved wife that adorned the walls. It was evident he held her memory dear to his heart. Our conversation touched on a range of topics, and he was particularly interested in hearing my story about why I needed a place to sleep. I opened up to him and shared my journey, revealing I was a Christian. He spoke at length about himself and his wife, regaling me with tales of their shared experiences. However, he also confided that after her passing, he struggled with depression and had gave up their home. He had opted to live a simpler life in the back of the store, yet he couldn't escape the overwhelming sense of loss and longing for her.

Moved by his story, I shared with him some scriptures that had provided me comfort and strength during difficult times, such as 2 Corinthians 4:17. "For our light affliction," I shared, "which is but for a moment, worketh for us a far more exceeding and eternal weight of glory." These words from the Apostle Paul seemed to bring him solace, and we spoke at length about our mutual faith in God.

The night wore on, and I realized it was nearly midnight. At 11:30, I asked if I could rest for the night. He kindly directed me to select a mattress and promised to bring me a blanket and pillow. After finding a cozy and supportive mattress, I lay down and felt the exhaustion of the day overtake me. Before long, he emerged and approached my bedside.

Suddenly I felt the weight of another person on the mattress beside me. He had climbed up next to me!

I glanced over my shoulder at him, frowning. "Are you okay?" I asked.

"Yes, of course," he said. "I'm just enjoying our conversation; it's very enjoyable."

I rolled over and managed a polite smile. "Thank you for your company, but I'm exhausted and need to rest now."

"Of course," he said. "I'm quite tired as well."

He didn't move. What did this guy think was about to happen?

"Well, have a good night's sleep in the back of the store," I said, trying to give him a hint.

He tilted his body slightly towards me and made a polite request, "Would you be interested in sharing a sleeping space with me tonight and keeping each other company?"

I couldn't believe what I was hearing. I desperately needed a place to sleep and didn't want to resort to sleeping in my car. But there was no way I was going to trade physical intimacy for a bed.

"Thank you for the offer," I said, "but I'm afraid I can't share a sleeping space with anyone."

"I don't see why not," he said, pressing the issue. "You seem like a great person. I miss my wife terribly, and I know this may seem out of character, however, I thought since I am helping you, perhaps we could help each other."

I sat up, but my heart sank. "No," I replied as firmly as possible. "I am not interested in anything like that. I just want to sleep! I'm sorry."

"You're not being very grateful," he persisted, scowling at me. "We really connected during our conversation and had an enjoyable time together. After all, I have offered you a place to stay. It would be nice if we could at least... you know... snuggle together."

I leaped out of bed, feeling a sharp twist in my lower back, but I ignored it.

"No," I declared. "I understand you miss your wife, but I am not interested in anything like that."

He looked like he was about to pressure me again, so I continued, saying, "I can't believe you would even suggest such a thing. I am struggling through a tough time right now, and all I want is a place to sleep. Why would you try to take advantage of me?"

I grabbed my backpack off the floor. I didn't know where I would go, but I had to get away from this man and his foul exchange.

"Where are you intending to go?" he asked.

"I honestly don't know," I said. "It's too late to find anyone else to help me, and I am really hurt by this."

He climbed off the bed and held up his hands as if surrendering. "Don't leave, please. I—I'm sorry. I shouldn't have offered—asked—"

"I'm not going to sleep next to you," I said.

"I understand," he said. "I'll go back to my own space and leave you alone. I promise."

I stared at him, trying to detect a bluff. "Are you

absolutely sure? All I want to do is get some rest. If you try anything, I will leave immediately."

"I won't... *try* anything," he promised, as if the words hurt him to speak. "Please just lay down, and I'll—I'll go back and won't bother you."

I took the bag off my shoulder and slowly approached the mattress.

"Thank you," I said.

"You're welcome."

"Good night."

He turned toward his living quarters. "Good night to you too," he said.

Finally, after what seemed like an eternity, he vanished into his tiny apartment.

I lay on the bed and balled my hands into fists. The nerve of that man! How dare he attempt such a thing!

But I needed rest, both in body and spirit, so I whispered a prayer God would give me the grace to forgive my host for his sins. Then I begged for protection so I could actually sleep without fear of yet another violation of my person.

The Lord provided.

I slept soundly through the night, and the man didn't emerge from his back area until morning.

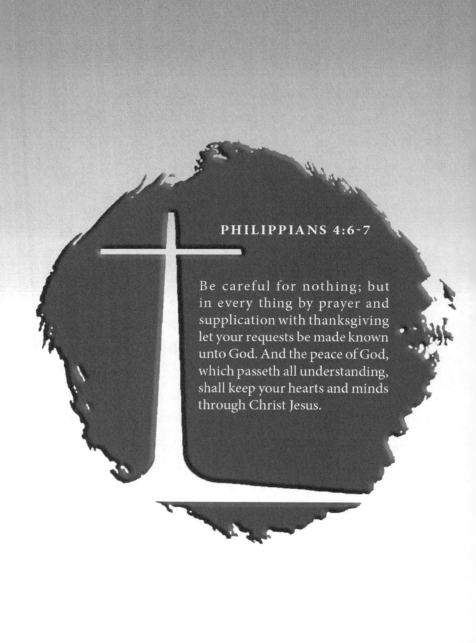

**PHILIPPIANS 4:6-7**

Be careful for nothing; but in every thing by prayer and supplication with thanksgiving let your requests be made known unto God. And the peace of God, which passeth all understanding, shall keep your hearts and minds through Christ Jesus.

## *Have You Considered*

---

## How Gratitude Can Ease
## Our Worst Sufferings?

HOMELESSNESS WAS UNDOUBTEDLY one of the most challenging experiences I've ever faced. It was incredibly lonely and humbling. It often left me feeling ashamed and humiliated, especially when people who knew me in my prior business life discovered what had become of me. Moreover, it was painful to see some friends with the resources to help chose not to.

This experience taught me to appreciate small acts of kindness from unexpected sources. It reminded me of Jesus' words in Matthew 25:40: "...Verily I say unto you, Inasmuch as ye have done it unto one of the least of these my brethren, ye have done it unto me." When we give our food, water, clothing, or time to those in need, Jesus makes it clear we do those acts unto Him. While most friends, for various reasons, didn't assist me, a handful of other friends and strangers periodically did show me kindness. Their thoughtful acts kept me going and helped me see there still is goodness in the world.

God's desire for me was to rely solely on Him and nothing else. In pursuit of this mission, He humbled me and stripped away everything I had placed my trust in. Throughout this transformative process, God imparted some of the most invaluable lessons one could learn in life. The trials of that challenging period fostered growth in ways that aligned perfectly with God's plan for me. Without facing these difficulties, I am uncertain whether I would have developed into the person He has me to be.

I am now grateful to God for this *gift* of a season of homelessness. Yes, I view it as a gift from God. It granted me a profound understanding of the challenges others endure, and I have acquired an understanding not to pass judgment on those facing similar struggles. When I encounter someone who is homeless, I make an effort to share my story and offer words of grace and encouragement. I remind them even in difficult circumstances, God can work in mysterious ways and use these experiences to shape their character and draw them close to Christ.

The most significant lesson I learned from my time of homelessness, which continues to guide me, revolves around prioritizing my life: God first, people second, and myself last. I've come to realize when I place God at the center of my life and make myself available to assist others, the results always are blessings beyond imagination. God's grace has consistently been abundant in my life, and I've witnessed firsthand how faithful He is to His promises. When I obediently follow the guidance of His Word and place others' needs ahead of mine, I am amazed at how my needs are met in the most extraordinary ways. I've come to understand life isn't about me; life is about God, and loving the people around me. When I keep my priorities in order—God first and others second—I experience genuine happiness and contentment in the midst of this bewildering journey of life.

Another invaluable lesson I gained is the importance of being grateful, especially in the midst of suffering. I know it may seem counterintuitive to express thanksgiving when faced with daunting circumstances; still, this experience illuminated my understanding of the immense power of offering gratitude to God during adversity. It taught me in the face of tragedies, we have the opportunity to turn them into times for the Lord to reveal His presence and grace.

In the face of suffering, we *need* to give thanks to God. Thanksgiving goes beyond mere religious obligation; rather, it's a mindset that can transform how we deal with pain. Giving thanks can alleviate our hearts and uplift our spirits amid hardships, shifting our focus from dwelling on struggles to acknowledging the blessings we still have. This change in perspective enables us to discover moments of comfort and hope, providing a glimmer of light to guide us through the toughest of times. Choosing to express thanksgiving fosters resilience and inner strength, nurturing a sense of hope and faith that fuels our determination to overcome adversity. It opens our hearts to sense God's peace and acceptance, helping us find meaning even in the most overwhelming challenges, and to endure and find the courage to persevere.

Furthermore, being grateful *in* suffering can lead to a profound sense of connection with God and others. Gratitude allows our hearts to embrace the peace of God, which possesses the remarkable capacity to flood our souls with profound intimacy. It also serves as a reminder we are not alone in our struggles and countless others are facing similar hardships. This shared experience connects us to the broader human condition and strengthens our empathy and compassion for others.

It is crucial to remember being grateful *in* suffering does not undermine the validity of our pain or the need for support and healing. Instead, it is an acknowledgment that amid the trials and tribulations, there are still elements of goodness and blessings to be found. Gratitude helps us to navigate the darkest corners of life with hope and a renewed sense of purpose.

Moreover, these lessons have enabled me to bear witness to remarkable displays of kindness and divine intervention. A whole book could be written with countless stories of how God has consistently met my needs in the most extraordinary and unexpected ways. Here are just a handful of examples:

Once, I found myself in urgent need of water. I paused to pray, asking God to provide me with a bottle of water. When I opened my eyes and happened to turn to the right, there was a new plastic bottle of water on the floor.

Another instance while waiting for a flight at the airport in Washington D.C., en route to do ministry work in Africa, a kind woman gave me $500 to support my endeavors. Unbeknownst to her, I was in dire need of that money.

Similarly, on a flight, I was seated next to an older woman who spent much of the journey in quiet prayer. Unexpectedly, she handed me a $100 bill and told me she felt moved by the Holy Spirit to give it to me.

And recently, a long-lost friend who I hadn't spoken to in over two decades reached out to me when I needed it most. During the call, she graciously electronically sent me all the funds I needed to purchase a flight back to the United States for an emergency.

Through the experience of homelessness, I came to understand God is indeed our Provider, and He yearns to be permitted to be involved in the details of our days. Life often tempts us with enticing distractions and false sources of happiness, but they are fleeting and perishing away. In stark contrast, the Lord remains true to His character and unwavering in His promises; He is the same yesterday, today, and forever regardless of our circumstances or decisions. He eagerly desires to be the sole object of our trust and devotion, offering us the steadfast anchor we need in a world of uncertainties.

By surrendering my career, comfortable home, and respected status in San Diego, I seemingly lost "everything" in the eyes of the world. However, in placing my trust in the One who holds the power to provide abundantly beyond my needs, I gained everything that truly matters. The journey wasn't easy, but it was undeniably sacred, and for that, I am immensely grateful!

I sincerely hope you won't have to go through the challenges I faced during my journey of homelessness. However, no matter the difficult trials God may allow you to encounter, my deepest desire for you is to experience the profound blessings that come from placing your complete trust and reliance in God for everything. The Lord has promised you good. Are you ready to lean entirely on the King of Kings for your provision? Can you wholeheartedly put your trust in Christ Jesus?

Take time to pray earnestly on this matter. Commit every aspect of your life to the Lord, and earnestly seek the courage to obey His guidance discovered in His Bible.

Then walk, trusting His ways are good, and He will not abandon you.

PSALM 34:18

The LORD is nigh unto them that are of a broken heart; and saveth such as be of a contrite spirit.

# *Thirteen*

---

# The Lord Is Near to You

IS GOD A GOOD GOD? Is my suffering a sign of His love or His hate? Why are awful things happening to me or to those I love?

These questions will follow us until we draw our final breath. As we've witnessed, every moment spent in this world is subject to Satan's corrupting power. We eagerly await Christ's return, for in eternity, all death will cease, all evil will be banished, and every tear will be wiped away from our eyes.

As of this writing, that day is yet to come. For now, we must endure the trials and tribulations of this life.

But we do not endure them alone. Our Lord took on flesh and became like unto us, suffering physical pain, emotional distress, spiritual anguish, social slander, temptation to sin, and utter rejection.

Scripture is lush with reminders God has a special place in his heart for those who suffer. David wrote in Psalm 34:18-19, "The LORD is nigh unto them that are of a broken heart; and saveth such as be of a contrite spirit. Many are the afflictions of the righteous: but the LORD delivereth him out of them all."

Afflictions are coming. They troubled David over three millennia ago; they oppressed Paul during his ministry two thousand years ago; they constantly frustrate my life and yours. A life of suffering is not a sign of God's absence or judgment. They are a sign you are of this Earth.

The question is what you do with your suffering.

Do you struggle and strive to hide it, vanquish it, or deflect it onto others? Do you numb and medicate it with all manner of food, drink, and pleasure? Do you blame it on others and engage in a relentless campaign of justice, in which you are judge and jury?

Or do you entrust it to the One who suffered like us?

Only Jesus can make suffering beautiful. Only He can give it a purpose. Only Jesus can take death on the cross and upend the natural order of things.

To transform our approach to suffering, we must look at Jesus more. Look at Him as long as you can and as deeply as you can. Only by beholding Him, His Word, and His glory can we shed light on all the darkness around us.

How do we do this?

Establishing a concrete plan of action that places Jesus

at the core of your life is essential. That means scheduling and detailing how you will study Him, listen to Him, worship Him, and follow Him. By doing so, you will strengthen your discipline and empower yourself to take control of your busy life and center them on what truly matters. If you practice this and repeat it daily, you will develop healthy spiritual disciplines, leading to a more hopeful mindset and a trusting heart in God's guidance.

To get started, consider asking yourself the following questions:

• When in my day can I read God's Word?

• How will I ensure I can see and easily access God's Word wherever I am?

• How will I respond to the Word? (Journaling, prayer, meditation, obedience, etc.)

• When in my day can I pause and pray, re-centering myself on His ways and purposes?

• What words of Jesus can I display in my workspace so I'm regularly aligned with His heart?

• What distractions tend to pull my mind and heart away from dependence on Jesus? How can I minimize or schedule time for them apart from time with the Lord?

- What hobbies do I enjoy? How can I add prayer to these activities so I can do them for Christ's glory?

- What am I good at? How can I create reminders to pray for dependence and trust in these areas so I avoid falling into pride and independence from God?

- What biblical church do I submit to? How can I serve it more sacrificially with my time, treasure, and talent?

- What mentors around me know me well enough to speak into my life with convicting authority?

Doubtless, there are many more questions you can ask yourself as you redesign your life to depend on Jesus. These questions serve as an excellent starting point, urging you to shift your strength and dependence away from yourself and onto God. We are so prone to seek refuge from life's struggles in our wealth, safety, comfort, and pride, but in doing so, we miss the opportunity to receive sustenance from the source of all life itself, the Lord God Almighty. Your needs don't grieve this God; He craves them. He longs to provide for you and is jealous when you seek provision elsewhere.

By persisting in practicing these wise practices, you will undoubtedly learn valuable lessons and gain wisdom that will prove beneficial as you navigate new opportunities and challenges. Only by depending on the Lord Jesus Christ can we find true peace and contentment amidst a life rife with suffering. Through this dependence, we find the strength to overcome and the resilience to thrive in the face of adversity.

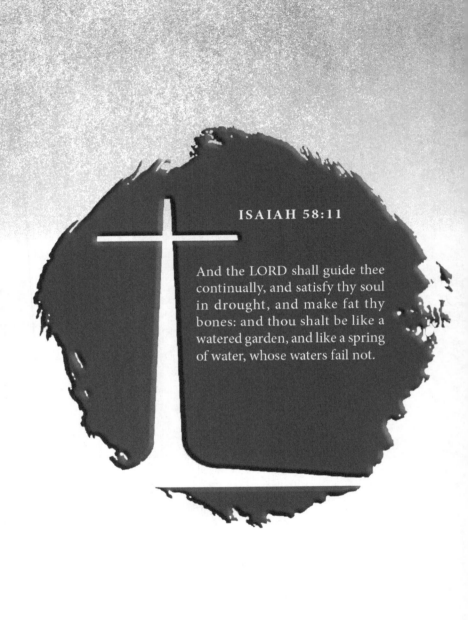

ISAIAH 58:11

And the LORD shall guide thee
continually, and satisfy thy soul
in drought, and make fat thy
bones: and thou shalt be like a
watered garden, and like a spring
of water, whose waters fail not.

## *Fourteen*

# My Prayer for You

IT'S SO EASY TO FORGET the nature of the gospel. Weakness is strength. Poverty is wealth. Humility is glory.

All of this is possible because of the atoning sacrifice of Jesus Christ, the Son of Man, who died on the cross for the sins of all and rose again to life. By adopting His humble demeanor, we receive His incredible glory, all because of what He did.

The writings of the Apostle Paul reminds us of this new paradigm in 2 Corinthians, boasting about his weaknesses because he understood it was only through his weakness that the power of Christ rested upon him: "…for when I am weak, then am I strong" (2 Corinthians 12:10).

Like Paul, we must learn to find joy in our weaknesses, necessities, and distresses. Only by resting in Christ can we learn to accept and embrace the sorrows and adversities God assigns to us. In doing so, we can experience Christ's power in our lives.

Therefore, we should not reject God's sovereignty over our lives but rather embrace it. We should recognize that grace and affliction are two sides of the same coin. As we make ourselves available to Christ, we accept and embrace our troubles. By decreasing our confidence in ourselves and increasing our confidence in God, we allow Christ to shine through our lives.

The Christian who is willing to let Christ's power rest upon him understands the value of embracing personal weaknesses. Instead of rejecting affliction, he finds joy in the opportunity to become weak so Christ should be magnified. By allowing ourselves to decrease and Christ to increase, we develop a deeper reliance on God and a stronger faith that can endure adversity, sorrow, or infirmity that comes our way. Ultimately, it is through embracing our weaknesses Christ becomes evident in our lives before others.

Indeed, God gives us the bread of adversity and the water of affliction (Isaiah 30:20). Troubles work to remove any independent, self-reliant mindset that could lead to overconfidence and stubbornness, and rather, they foster trust in the Lord within us. Just as Solomon proclaimed in Proverbs 3:5-6, "Trust in the LORD with all thine heart; and lean not unto thine own understanding. In all thy ways acknowledge him, and he shall direct thy paths." We must embrace the adversity and affliction God allows into our lives, recognizing they are ultimately for our good and will help us grow in our faith and trust Him.

Like Jesus, we must persevere through our adversities, griefs, and weaknesses, as these provide opportunities for the Lord to glorify Himself, and we should take notice. For what greater weakness was there than Christ hanging on the cross? And what greater glory could follow it than the Holy Spirit raising the deceased body of Jesus back to life?

God promises to supply us with grace through all manner of trials and troubles. Is it so we may boast about our toughness? No! It is for His honor so the Son of God should be glorified through us.

People are watching us, critical of rampant hypocrisy in the Christian church. Will we continue subscribing to worldly power structures, shunning weakness, and embracing political and economic strength? Or will we humble ourselves under the mighty hand of God and celebrate our struggles for the chance at dependence in Jesus Christ?

Our afflictions serve as a powerful testimony to unbelievers, demonstrating our hope in Jesus is a true and living hope. Through our perseverance in suffering, others may be drawn to believe in Christ, and He will be magnified. It is a wondrous mystery that by turning the conventional order of our world, we can win sinners to Christ!

Paul found joy in his afflictions because he was vigilant in observing how God worked through them for a greater purpose. He explained that even in the midst of unjust hardships affecting him and his mission teams, these challenges were offering unique opportunities to share the gospel of Christ to more masses of people. His "bonds of afflictions" were moments for Christ to be exalted before unbelievers who watched his manner of life, sometimes in dark dungeons and difficult jailhouses. His steadfastness in the face of adversity flew in the face of conventional Greek and Roman culture. It stunned pagan cultists to repent and devote their lives to the one true God—Jesus Christ. Paul's sufferings opened doors for him to proclaim the message of Christ's death, burial, and resurrection for the forgiveness of sins. Therefore, he rejoiced in his afflictions and encouraged others to do the same.

May we embrace the strength and courage to follow his example!

Let us not nullify the grace of God that has been given to us. As believers, we have been made partakers of Christ if we remain steadfast in our confidence until the end. Therefore, let us not abandon our confidence, for it holds a promising reward.

We are promised God's presence here on Earth and His unending glory for all eternity in Heaven. We are sealed with the earnest of His Holy Spirit. We are adopted heirs of the Creator of the universe. What good and glorious news!

Until that day, however, we must endure. We must remain ever hopeful and watchful for the mighty hand of God in our lives. We must embrace weakness and neediness to fully receive the good gifts of our great God.

So let us hold firm, and, as Paul wrote to the Corinthians,

"...be ye steadfast, unmoveable, always abounding in the work of the Lord, forasmuch as ye know that your labour is not in vain in the Lord" (1 Corinthians 15:58).

Later, to the Galatians and his young disciple Timothy, "And let us not be weary in well doing: for in due season we shall reap, if we faint not. And the Lord shall deliver [us] from every evil work, and will preserve [us] unto his heavenly kingdom: to whom be glory for ever and ever. Amen" (Galatians 6:9; 2 Timothy 4:18).

This is my prayer for you.

I pray you do not grow weary in doing good for the Lord. I pray you find steadfast, immovable strength in the life, death, and resurrection of Jesus Christ.

And I pray you see beauty in your suffering, purposeful glory, entrusting you to an eternity of comfort and satisfaction in the arms of your beloved Saviour.

Dear Reader,

Have you enjoyed reading this book? If so, would you consider passing it along to someone who might need comfort and encouragement? As you hold this book in your hands, I want you to know it was written with the sole purpose of spreading hope and encouragement to all who read it.

I am convinced each of us carries a testimony that possesses the ability to uplift and help lives. That's why I'm committed to making this book available to as many people as possible through my ministry. By doing so, we can invest in the lives of others by sowing seeds of hope into countless hearts, even those we may never have the privilege to meet.

If you have found encouragement and inspiration within these pages, would you kindly consider supporting

my ministry? Your donations play an important role in two significant ways. First, they enable me to continue freely distributing copies of this book, as well as other books, to individuals around the world, reaching those who may be in need of a comforting message. Second, your generous support assists me in extending my reach further, allowing me to serve and minister to vulnerable individuals, particularly youngsters, showering them with the love and teachings of our Lord Jesus Christ.

If you wish to make a donation, kindly visit MissionFrontier.info and click on the "Donate" or "Book Angels" tabs. Your compassionate gift holds great value to me, and I am deeply grateful for your prayers and generosity.

With gratitude,

Dear Leader,

As I conclude my memoir, I am filled with profound gratitude for the opportunity to share my journey of faith in Christ and the hope that has sustained me through times of suffering. I earnestly hope my experiences can offer solace and encouragement to those facing their trials.

If you find resonance in the content of my memoir and believe my testimony could edify your community, then I welcome you to reach out to me through my ministry's website www.MissionFrontier.info. If there's a way I can be of support or assistance, it would be a genuine blessing to serve your community. I am committed to seeking God in prayer concerning any communication.

My passion revolves around exalting the Lord Jesus Christ while serving others through the complexities of their journeys. It's a privilege to speak with others, listen, and learn from others' stories, and together, seek God's wisdom and comfort amidst life's challenges.

May Christ Jesus be the preeminence of your lives as we should continually grow in faith, hope, and charity through the ever-changing seasons of life. May God's grace and favor be a constant presence as you dedicate your endeavors to exalt Christ and minister to others.

In Christ's service,

# Children's Books Available!

## in English and Spanish!

www.WaymakerPublishing.com

**CRAVING MORE EXCEPTIONAL READS?** Discover a treasury of captivating books by outstanding authors, including a rich collection of Lawrence's works. Your next great adventure awaits at www.WaymakerPublishing.com to order your copies– start exploring today!

**Inspired by a true story, 'Left Alive' is a gripping tale of love and survival.**

A single mother's second chance at love turns tragic when her charming boyfriend turns violent. Shot and left comatose, her journey showcases the power of instincts and the importance of heeding warning signs. 'Left Alive' is a haunting yet hopeful account of faith, family, and perseverence in the face of darkness.

**The light is exposed to a harsh truth– Sex trafficking isn't just a foreign issue; it plagues America as well.**

This book challenges this myth, bringing together survivors, counselors, law enforcement, policymakers, and scholars to offer a comprehensive view of the problem. By uniting diverse perspectives, it outlines strategies to combat this illicit trade, fostering a collaborative approach to end modern slavery in all its forms.

**Are you searching for a life marked by success, prosperity, abundance, and fulfillment?**
If you answered 'yes,' then this book is for you! Lawrence unveils the riches and hope that awaits anyone who desires to be free from this world's chaos and despair. This stirring and thought-provoking book leads readers to unlock the promise of God that offers living life abundantly.

**This user-friendly handbook swiftly directs you to relevant Scriptures**
that address and confirm truths related to your questions and concerns. It offers uplifting guidance, empowering you to embrace your role as an effective soulwinner, in alignment with God's calling for you.

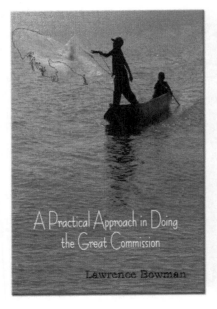

Practical *and* Effective
Methods
*for*
Sharing the Gospel

And [Jesus] said unto them, Go ye into all the world, and preach the gospel to every creature. And that repentance and remission of sins should be preached in his name among all nations, beginning at Jerusalem.
—Mark 16:15; Luke 24:47

Lawrence Bowman

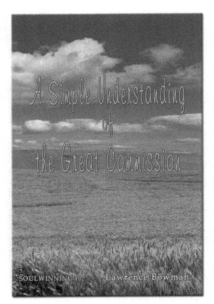

**"The Soulwinning Series," a guide to living a purposeful life aligned with the Savior's Great Commission.**

These books expound on a diverse array of practical and important topics: Can a Christian really use his ordinary life to accomplish God's purpose? How does one wield his influence for Christ? Discover the love of Gospel sharing and investing in discipleship. Join this transformative journey of empowerment and impact.

# Escape into a World of Relaxation

## with Lawrence's Captivating Adult Coloring Book!

Over 50 intricate pages await your creative touch, offering a therapeutic escape from stress. Featuring a diverse array of themes, perfect for all skill levels, and designed with no bleed-through worries, it's an ideal gift for any occasion. Unleash your inner artist and embark on a delightful coloring journey.

Made in the USA
Middletown, DE
23 June 2024

56014135R00152